Learn to Sing in Harmony Level One

English & Español Empathy Songs

Sarah Samuelson
STUDIO

www.sarahsamuelsonstudio.com

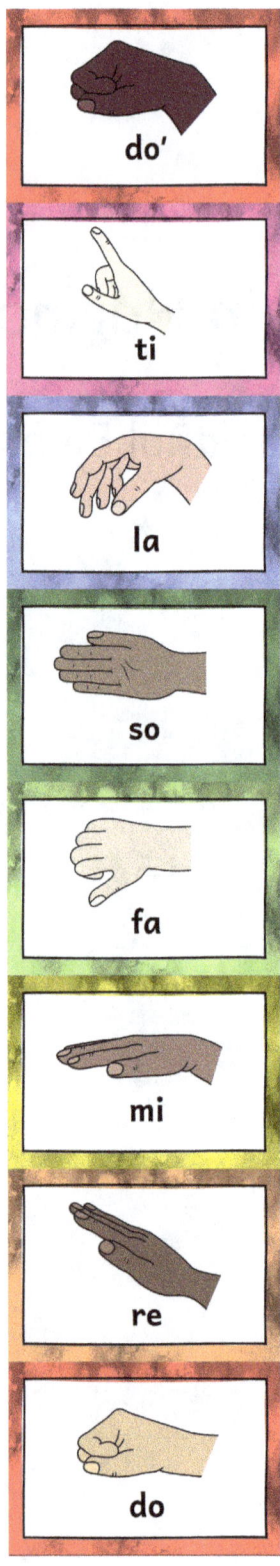

Copyright © 2024 Sarah Samuelson Studio
All Rights Reserved.

No part of this publication may be reproduced or transmitted in any form without permission from the publisher.

Learn to Sing in Harmony Level One Contents

do, C

1. Introduction to Rhythm — 1
2. We are Part of this Beautiful World — 5
   Español - Formamos Parte de este Hermoso Mundo — 7

do-re, C-D

3. I Have Worth — 8
   Español - Creo que tengo valor — 10
4. I Can Show Empathy — 11
   Español - Puedo mostrar empatía — 13

do-re-mi, C-D-E

5. Do-Re-Mi Body Tap — 14
   Words Can Be Healing to Say — 15
   Español - Las palabras tienen poder curativo — 16
6. Welcome Here   **harmony: round** — 17
   Español - Bienvenido aqui *(England: Hot Cross Buns)* & Hot Cross Buns — 19
7. I Can Be a Friend — 21
   Español - Puedo ser un amigo *(France: Au Clair de la Lune)* — 22
8. Leap for Joy — 23
   Español - Salta de Alegría *(USA: Hop Old Squirrel)* — 25
9. I Can Be More Understanding — 26
   Español - Puedo ser más comprensivo *(Spiritual: Babylon's Falling)* — 28

do-re-mi-so, C-D-E-G

10. Put Yourself in Their Shoes — 29
    Español - Ponte en su Lugar *(Spiritual: Oh, I'm Gonna to Sing)* — 31
11. We Want All to Feel Connected — 32
    Español - Queremos ke todos se sientan conectados *(USA: Mary Had a Little Lamb)* — 34
12. We Each Have a Family — 35
    Español - Cado uno tiene una familia *(USA: Johnny Works with One Hammer)* — 37
13. Little Changes Make a Difference — 38
    Español - Pequeños cambios marcan la diferencia *(Robert Lowry)* — 40

do-re-mi-fa-so, C-D-E-F-G

14. Our Voice is Important — 42
    Español - Nuestra voz importa *(Bohemian Folk Song)* — 44
15. Stay Hopeful — 45
    Español - Puedo tener esperanza — 47

Low so-la-do-re-mi-so, G-A-C-D-E-G

16. Care for My Neighbor — 48
    Español - Cuidar a mi Vecino *(Germany: Mäh, Lämmchen, Mäh)* — 50
17. We Want Justice in Our World — 51
    Español - Queremos Justicia en Nuestro Mundo *(Spiritual: Oh!Oh! Freedom)* — 53

do-re-mi-fa-so-la, C-D-E-F-G-A

18. You are Important — 54
    Español - Eres importante *(England: Here Comes a Bluebird)* — 56
19. We Can Learn to Express Our Emotions — 57
    Español - Aprendemos a expresar emociones *(Argentina: Los elefantes)* — 59
20. We are Like Stars in the Night — 60
    Español - Somos como estrella en la Noche *(France: Twinkle, Twinkle)* — 62
    English - Twinkle, Twinkle, Little Star — 63
    Español - Spanish Estrellita Donde Estas — 64
    Français - Ah! Vous dirai-je, Maman — 65
21. We all Have a Super Power — 66
    Español - Todos tenemos un superpoder *(Mexico: Chocolate molinillo)* — 68
22. I am Learning to Regulate   **harmony: round** — 69
    Español - Estoy aprendiendo a regularme *(Japan: Kaeru No Uta)* — 71
    Japanese - Kaeru No Uta — 72
    Chords & Intervals - Level 1 — 73

Copyright©2024 by Sarah Samuelson Studio
All rights reserved. Printed in the USA.

Introduction to Learn to Sing in Harmony

Learn to Sing in Harmony is a curriculum for learning how to read music by singing and help develop the skill and joy of singing harmony. The solfège method assigns each note in the music scale with a syllable: do-re-mi-fa-so-la-ti-do much as heard in the song "doe a deer...ray a drop of golden sun." This curriculum starts with songs only using do, then do-re, then do-re-mi and so on. Melodies are songs from different countries and African American spirituals. Here are some ways to utilize this method:

1) **Learn to read music notes by singing**
   a) Start with melodies you know like "Mary Had a Little Lamb" or "Twinkle Twinkle" and sing the melody in the solfège which is included in every song.
   b) Practice the hand signs that go with each note to help remember the solfège.
   c) Sing the language you are most familiar with then try other languages.
   d) Add your creativity! Once you've learned the song start improvising or creating your own version with new rhythms and tones! Remember the rhythms are only simplified for learning.
   e) Sing the songs with harmony. The first type of harmony is called a "round." Multiple people sing the same melody but start at different times. The starting places are indicated by numbers in the measure.

2) **Learn to read notes by playing Boomwhackers** – Boomwhackers are inexpensive and easy to play. There are eight colored tubes and each one labeled with a different pitch. The music notes in this book are the same colors. Every time you see a red "do" you tap the red Boomwhacker.

3) **Learn to play ukulele and piano chords** - Diagrams for the ukulele and piano chords are included on every page. This "beginner" book has only three chords that have so multiple songs have the same chords. Repetition of the same chords helps us learn!

4) **Learn about empathy** – These songs are great for teaching what it means to have empathy, understand emotions, and appreciate diversity.

5) **Learn different languages or reinforce English language learning** – Languages help retain culture! I include the International Phonetic Alphabet (IPA) to guide pronunciation of languages. This "alphabet" of sounds and symbols was developed to represent the various sounds that are similar in languages. However, the symbols do not convey the nuances and beauty of the languages, especially the ones that are tonal based like many in Africa. Listening to and learning from those who speak the language is always best. Honoring the languages of those around us brings harmony

6) **Continue learning more song, developing your ability to sing harmony, and understanding music theory and languages** to sing in choir or with small groups in Level 2, 3, 4 and more. If you have any questions contact info@sarahsamuelsonstudio.com. Happy singing!

Copyright©2024 by Sarah Samuelson Studio
All rights reserved. Printed in the USA.

Lesson 1: Rhythm - Walk, Jog & Rest

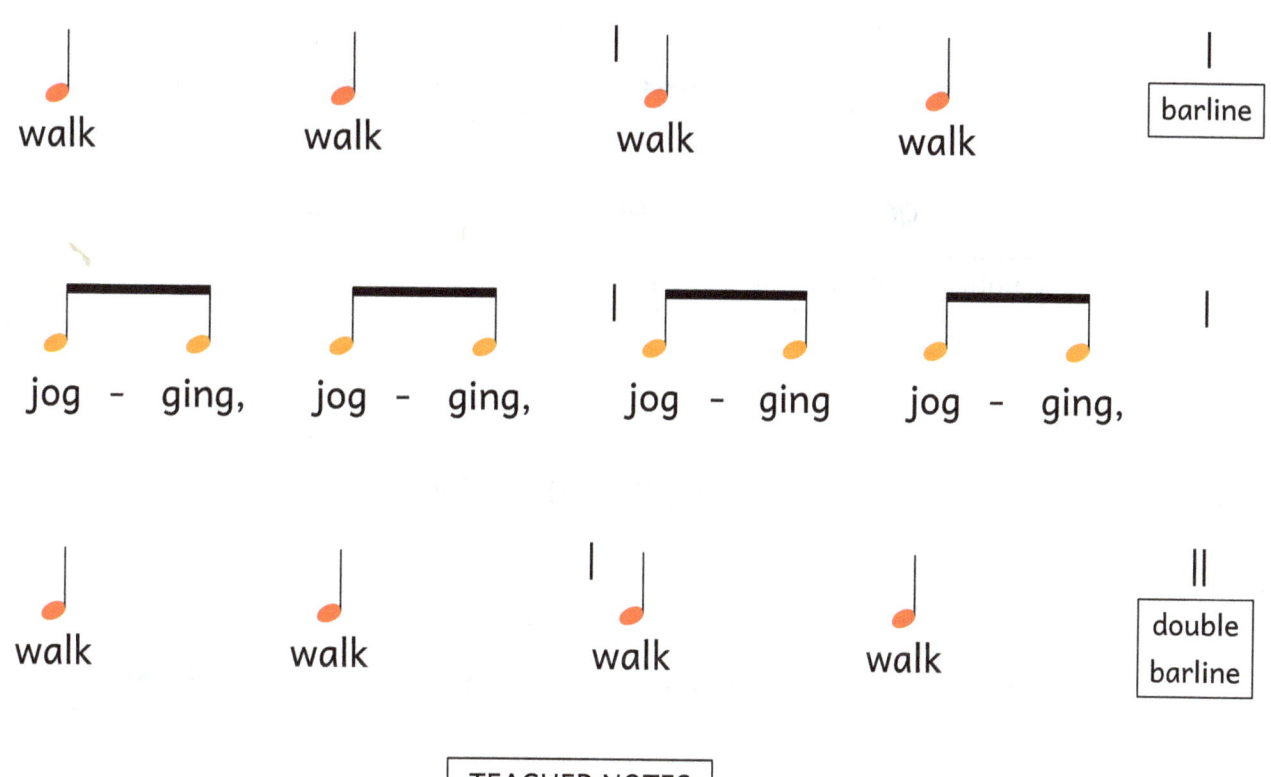

TEACHER NOTES

Speak the words in a steady beat to get to know the timing of the notes.
Speak the words as you walk and jog and keep a steady beat.

Copyright © 2024 Sarah Samuelson Studio

Rhythm in Speech

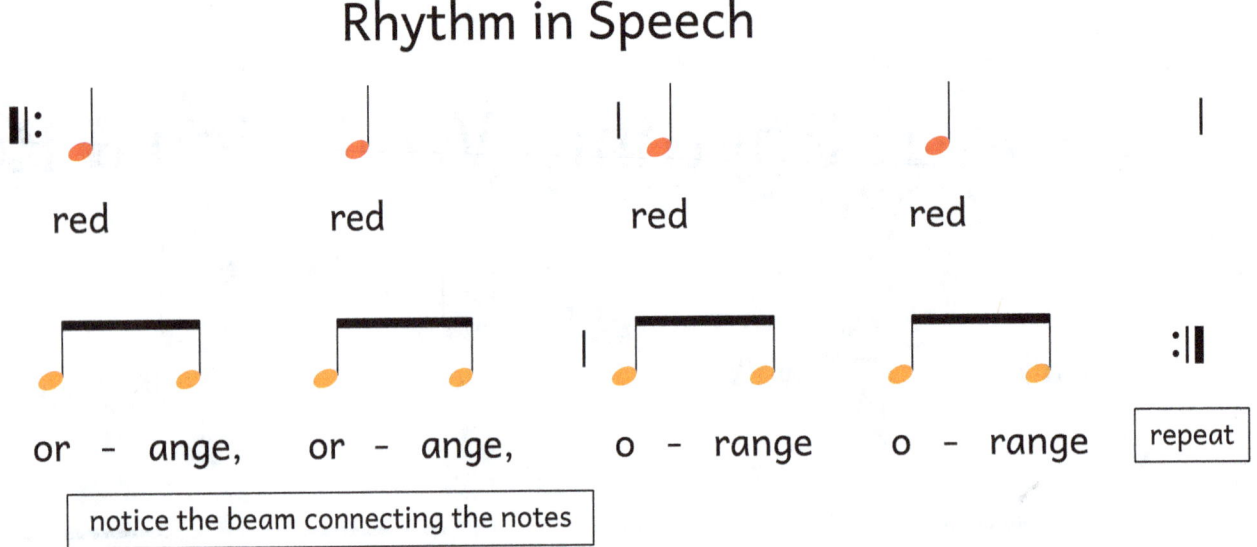

notice the beam connecting the notes

Rhythm in Silence

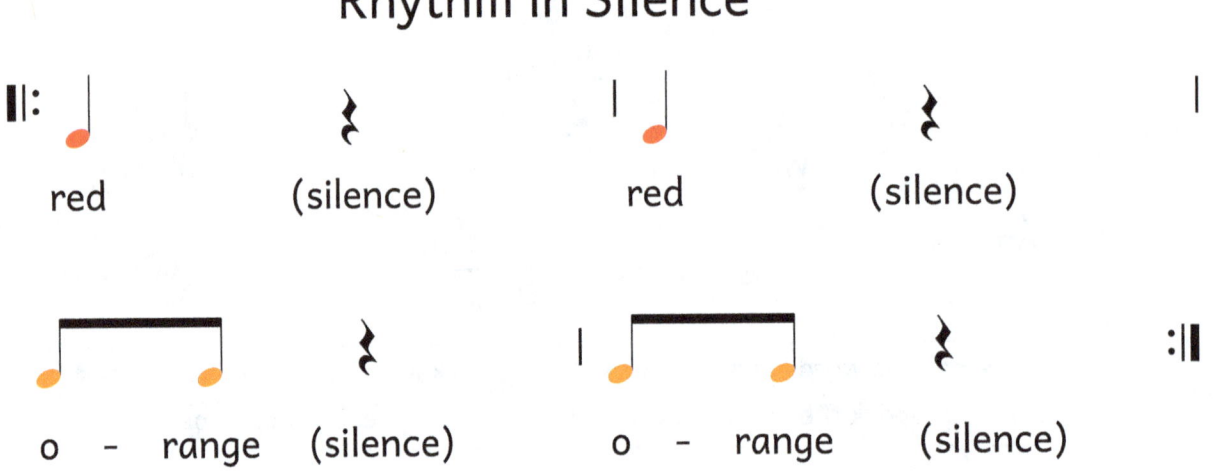

Copyright © 2024 Sarah Samuelson Studio

Quarter Notes

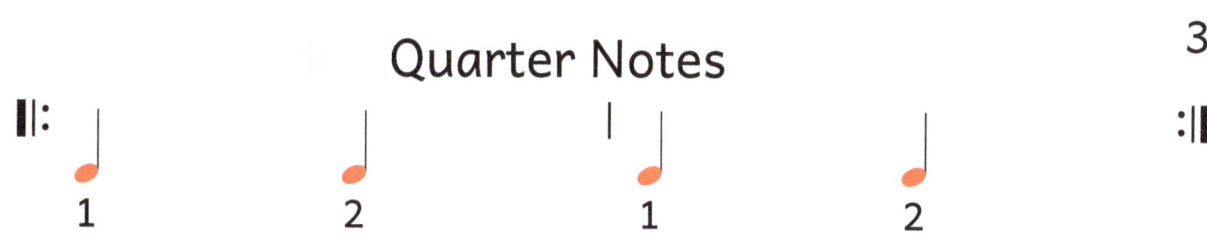

When counting quarter and eighth notes it is best to "subdivide" which means to add the "and" when counting the quarter notes so that your eighth notes can be more even.

Eighth Notes

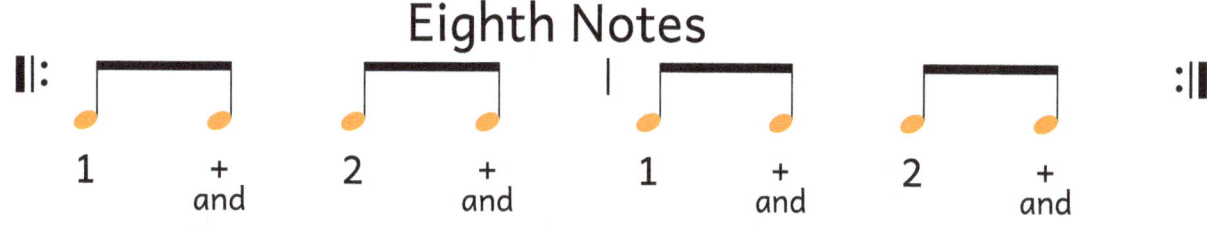

Quarter Notes & Rests

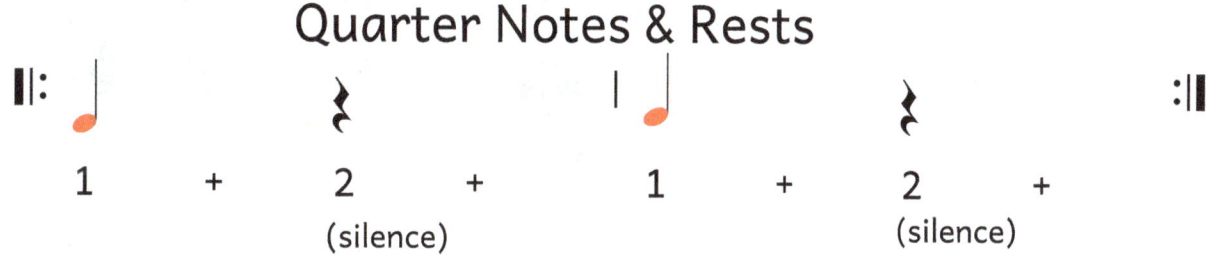

Eighth Notes & Rests

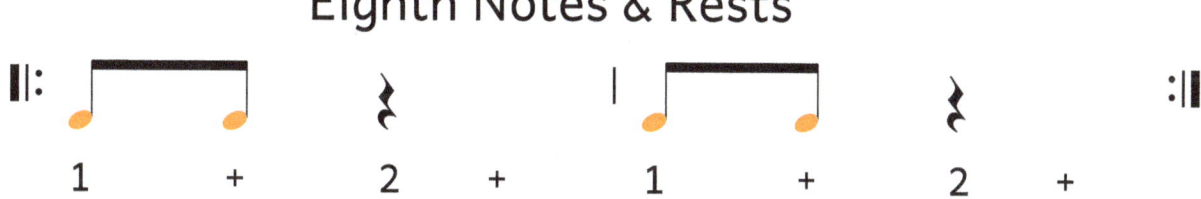

Quarter Notes & Eighth Notes & Rests

Copyright © 2024 Sarah Samuelson Studio

Solfège C Major Scale with Boomwhacker Colors

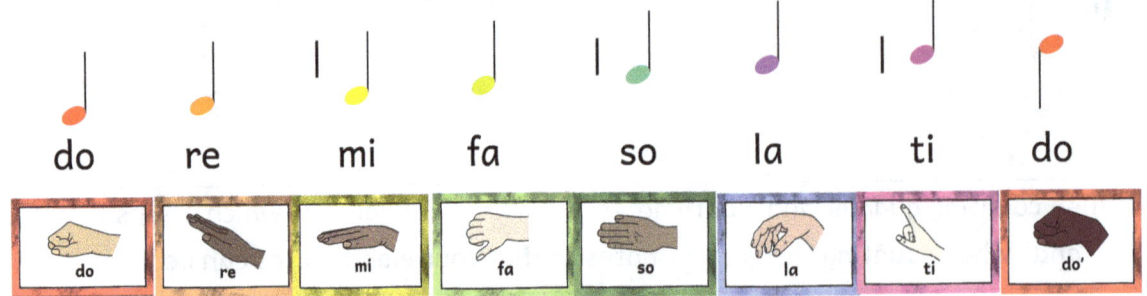

Solfège C Major Scale for Piano

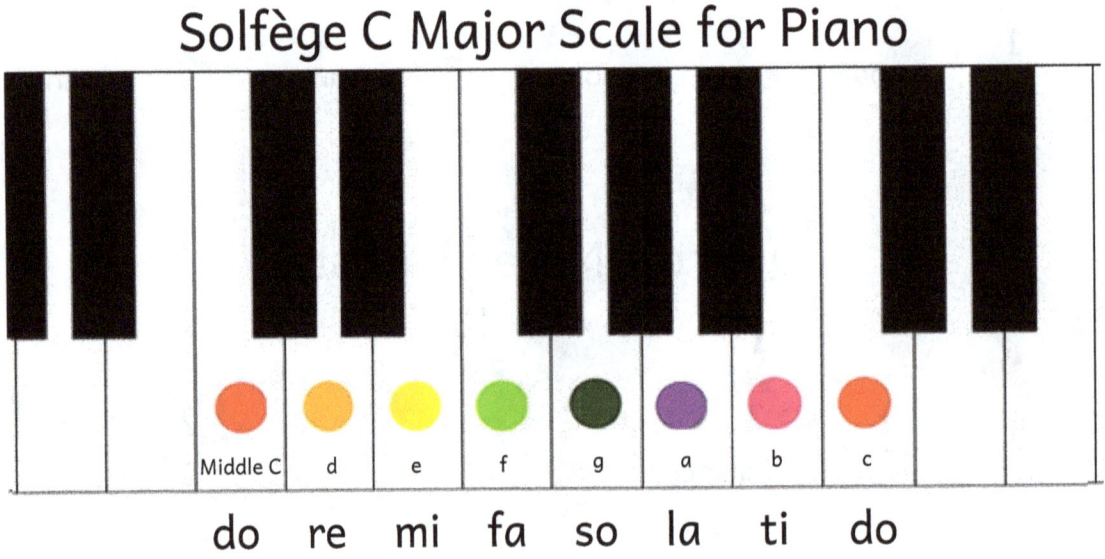

Chords for Piano

Lesson 2: do
We are Part of this Beautiful World
Music: Sarah Samuelson

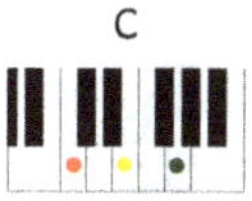

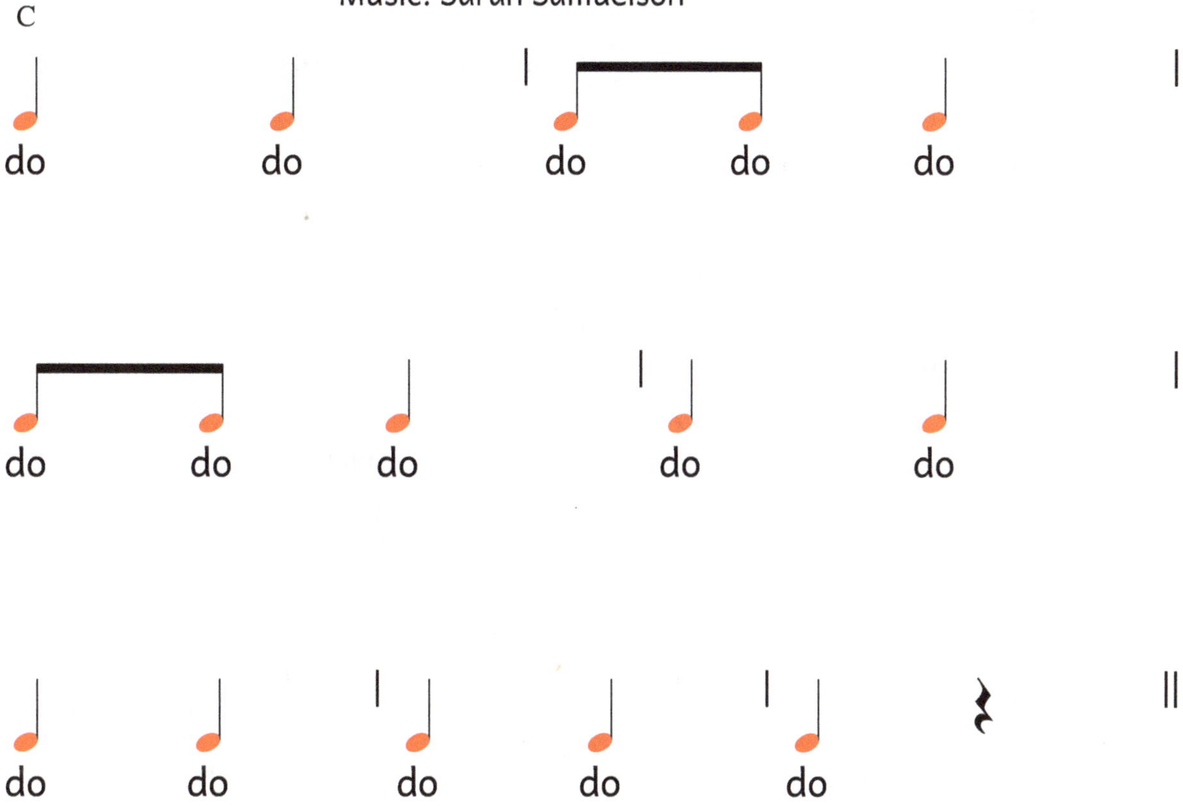

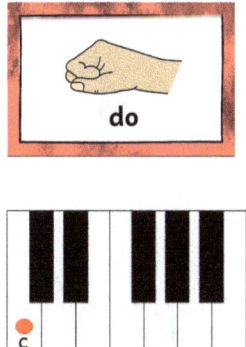

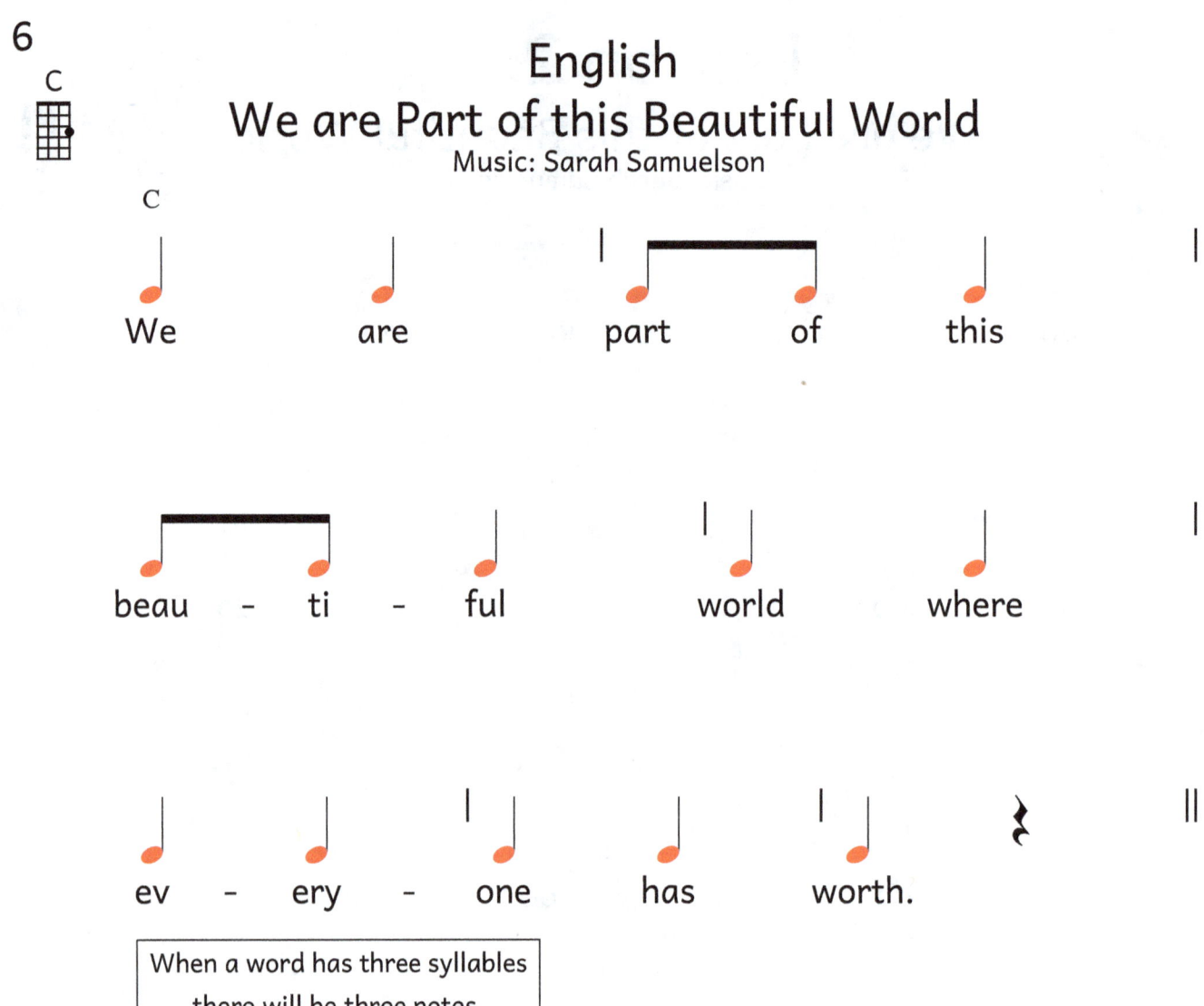

Español
Formamos Parte de Este Hermoso Mundo
Music: Sarah Samuelson

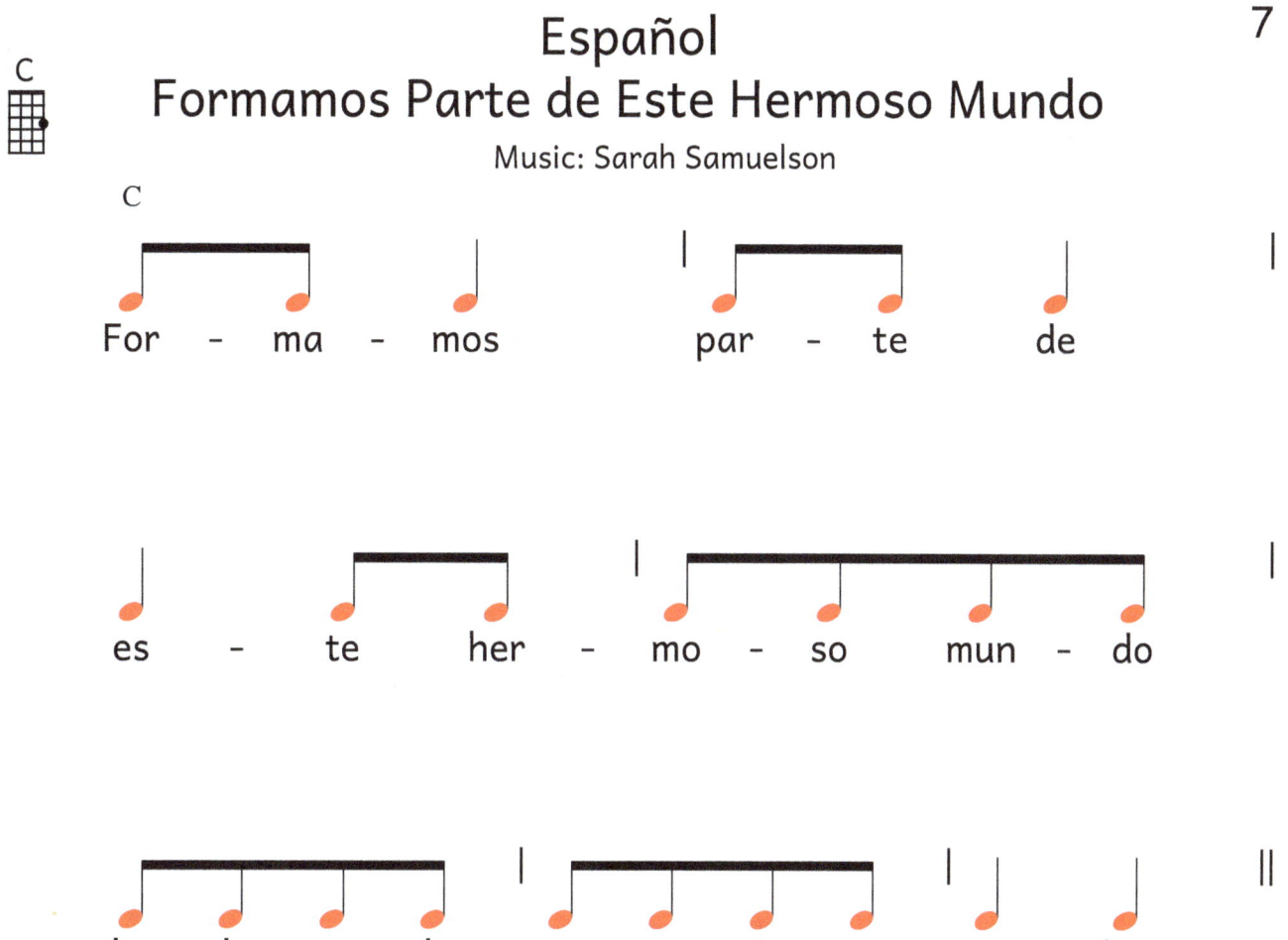

Español
Formamos parte de este hermoso mundo
donde cada uno tiene valor.

International Phonetic Alphabet
ˈfɔrmamos ˈparte ðe ˈeste erˈmoso ˈmundo
ˈdonde ˈkada ˈuno ˈtiene ˈba.lor.

Copyright © 2024 Sarah Samuelson Studio

Lesson 3: do-re
I Have Worth
Music: Sarah Samuelson

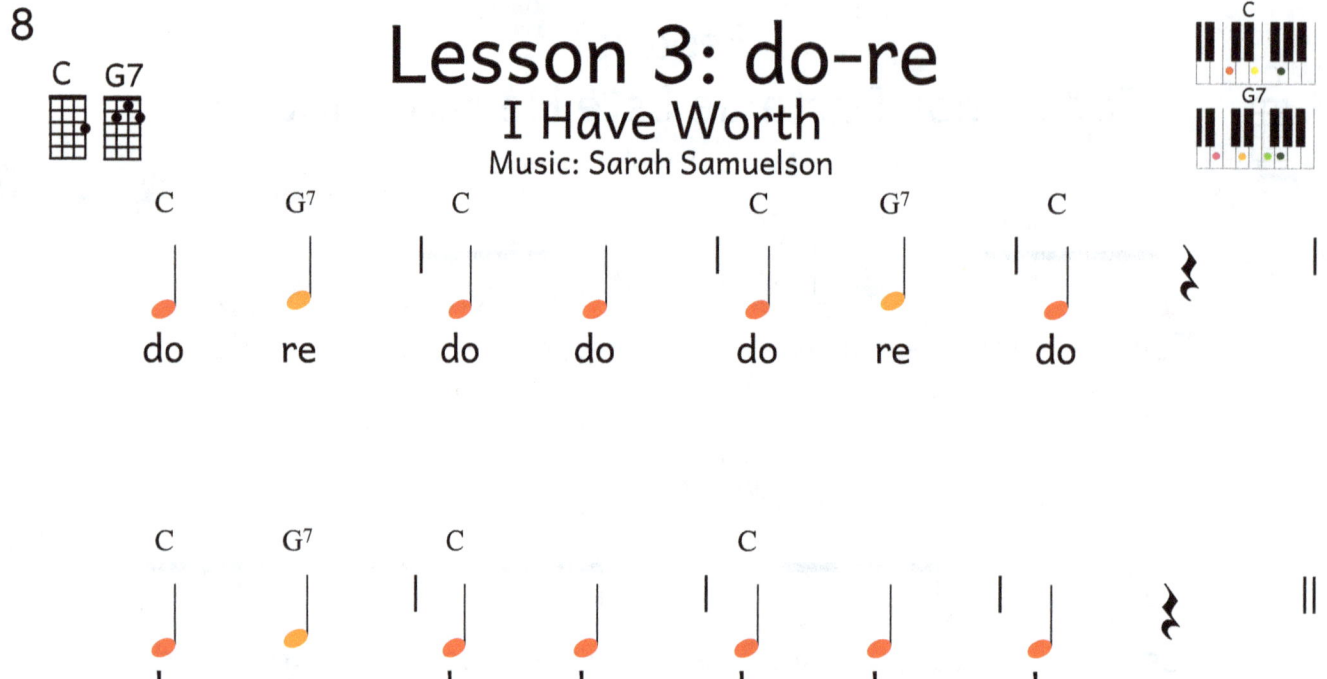

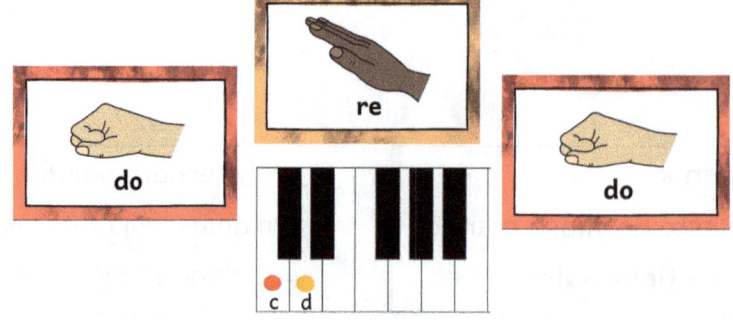

Copyright © 2024 Sarah Samuelson Studio

English
I Have Worth
Music: Sarah Samuelson

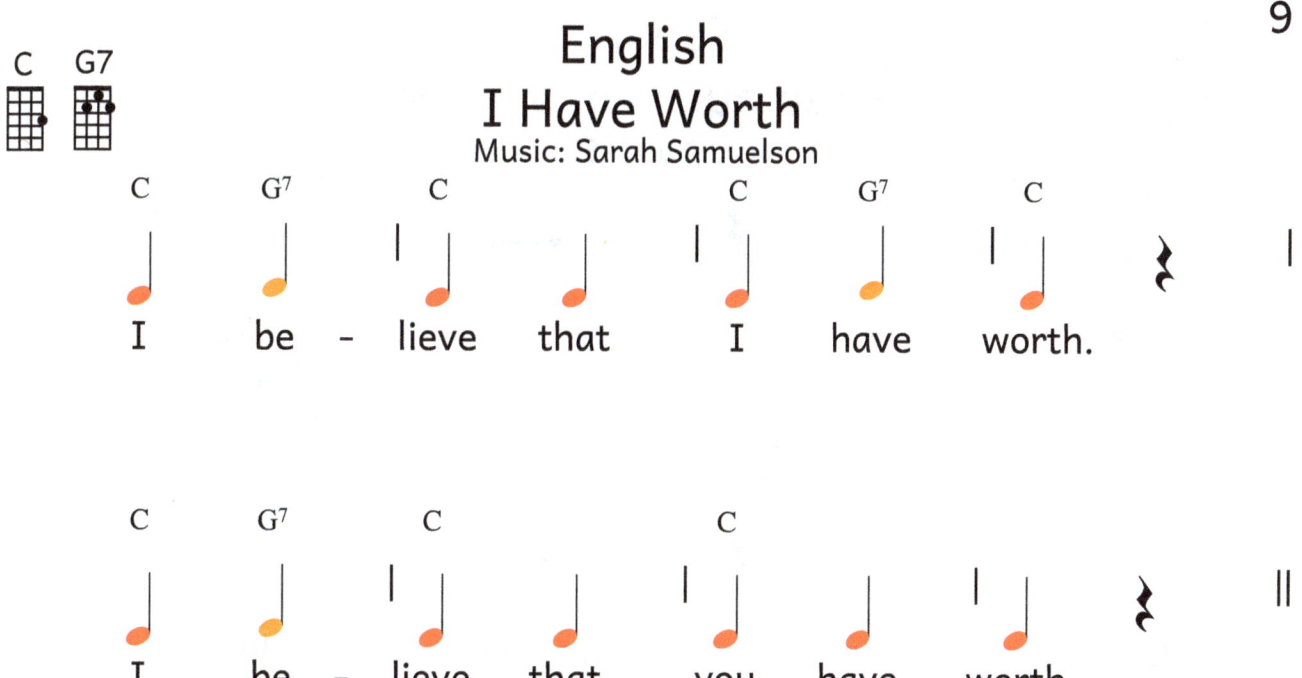

International Phonetic Alphabet
aɪ bɪˈliːv ðæt aɪ hæv wɜːrθ
aɪ bɪˈliːv ðæt juː hæv wɜːrθ

Actions
Walk around the classroom as you sing this song and point to others when singing, "You have worth."

Copyright © 2024 Sarah Samuelson Studio

Español	International Phonetic Alphabet
Creo que tengo valor	kreo ke ˈtengo βaˈlor.
Creo que tienes valor	ˈkreo ke ˈtjenes βaˈlor.

Copyright © 2024 Sarah Samuelson Studio

Lesson 4: do-re-do
I Can Show Empathy
Text & Music: Sarah Samuelson

C	C	G7	C	C	C	C	G7	C	C
do	do	re	do	do	do	do	re	do	do

C	C	G7	C	C	C	C	G7	C	C
do	do	re	do	do	do	do	re	do	do

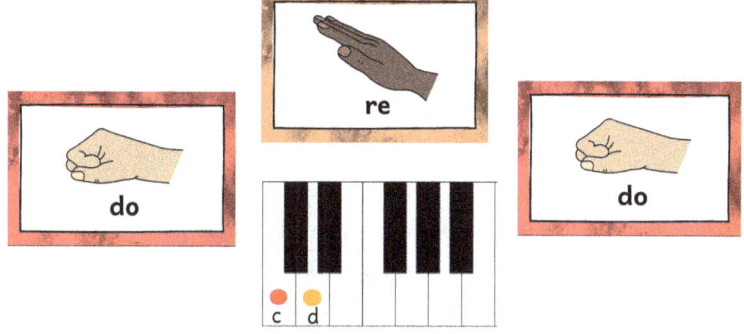

Copyright © 2024 Sarah Samuelson Studio

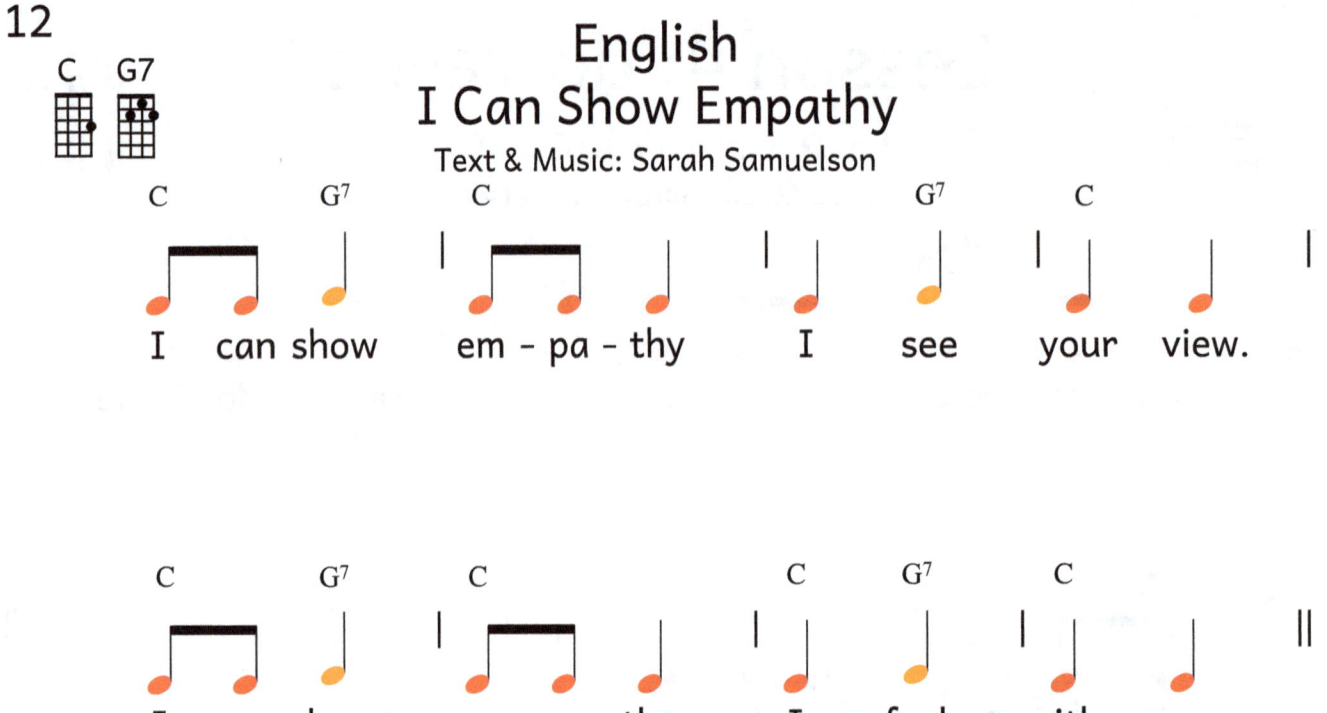

Español
Mostrar empatía
Music: Sarah Samuelson

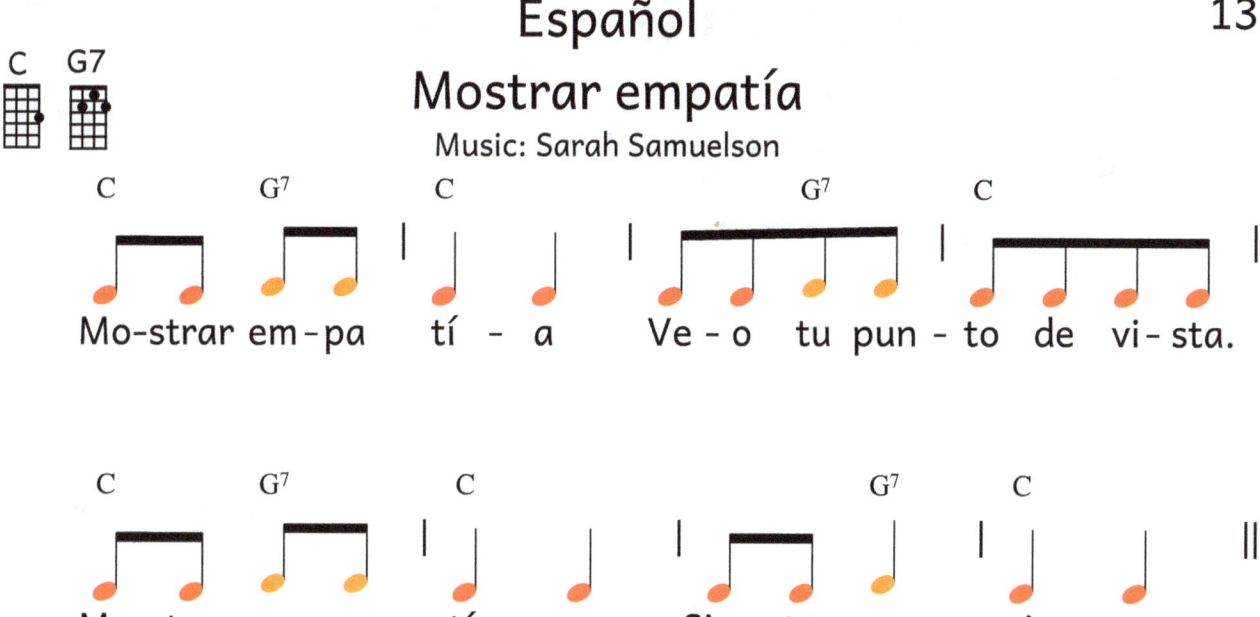

Español	International Phonetic Alphabet
Mostrar empatía.	mosˈtrar emˈpati.a
Veo tu punto de vista.	ˈbe.o tu ˈpunto de ˈbista
Mostrar empatía:	mosˈtrar emˈpati.a
Siento contigo.	ˈsjento konˈtiɣo

Copyright © 2024 Sarah Samuelson Studio

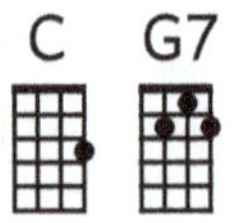

Lesson 5: do-re-mi
Do-Re-Mi Body Tap
Music: Sarah Samuelson

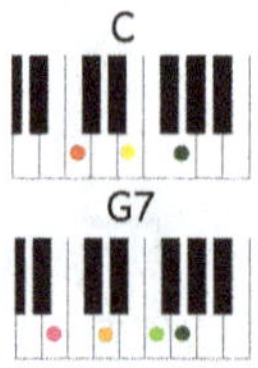

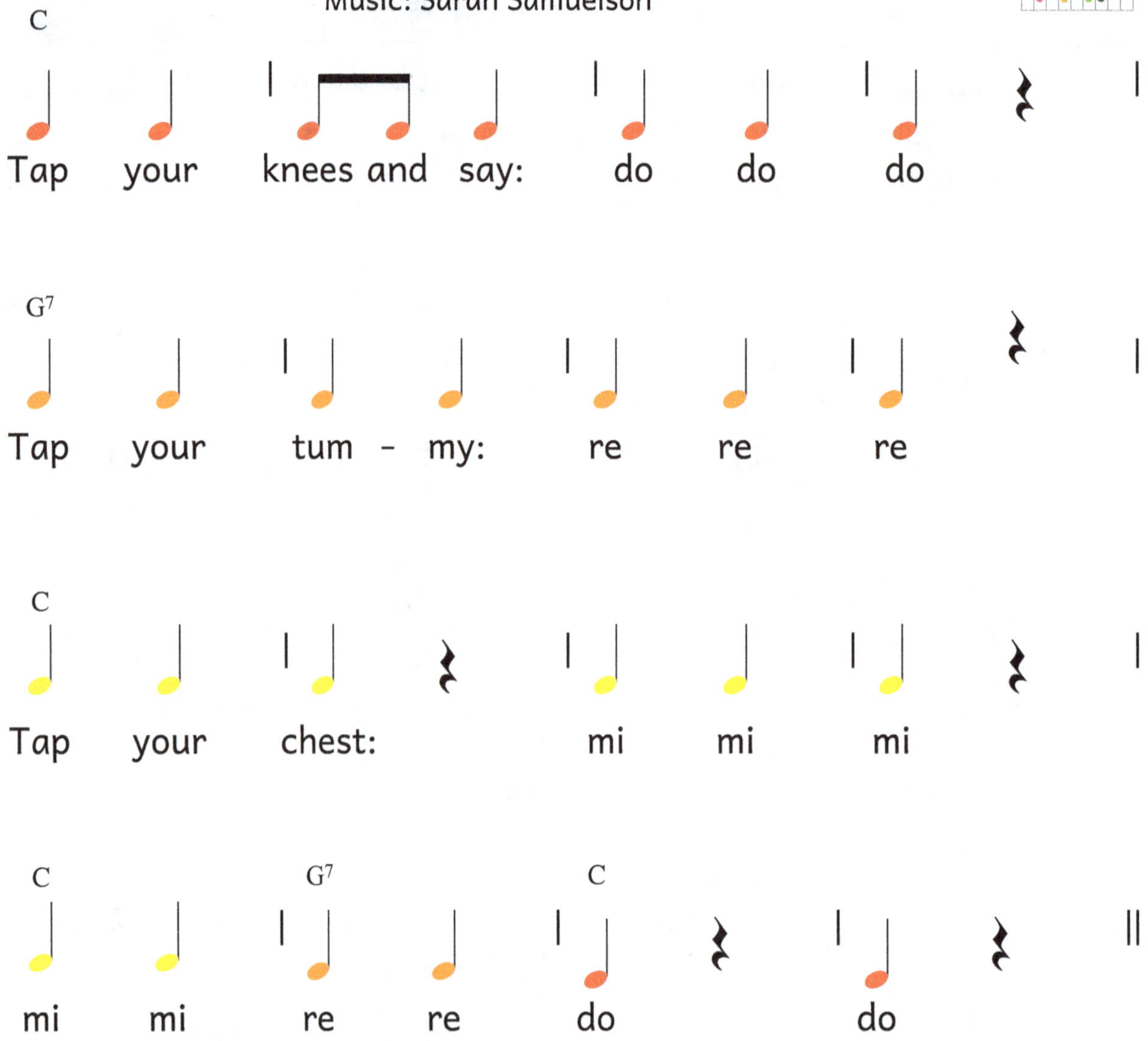

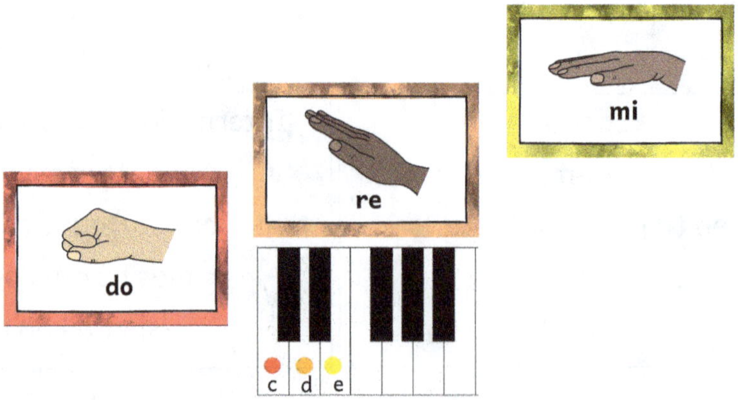

Tap your knees and say: do do do

Tap your tum - my: re re re

Tap your chest: mi mi mi

mi mi re re do do

Copyright © 2024 Sarah Samuelson Studio

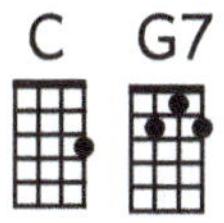

English
Words Can Be Healing to Say
Text & Music: Sarah Samuelson

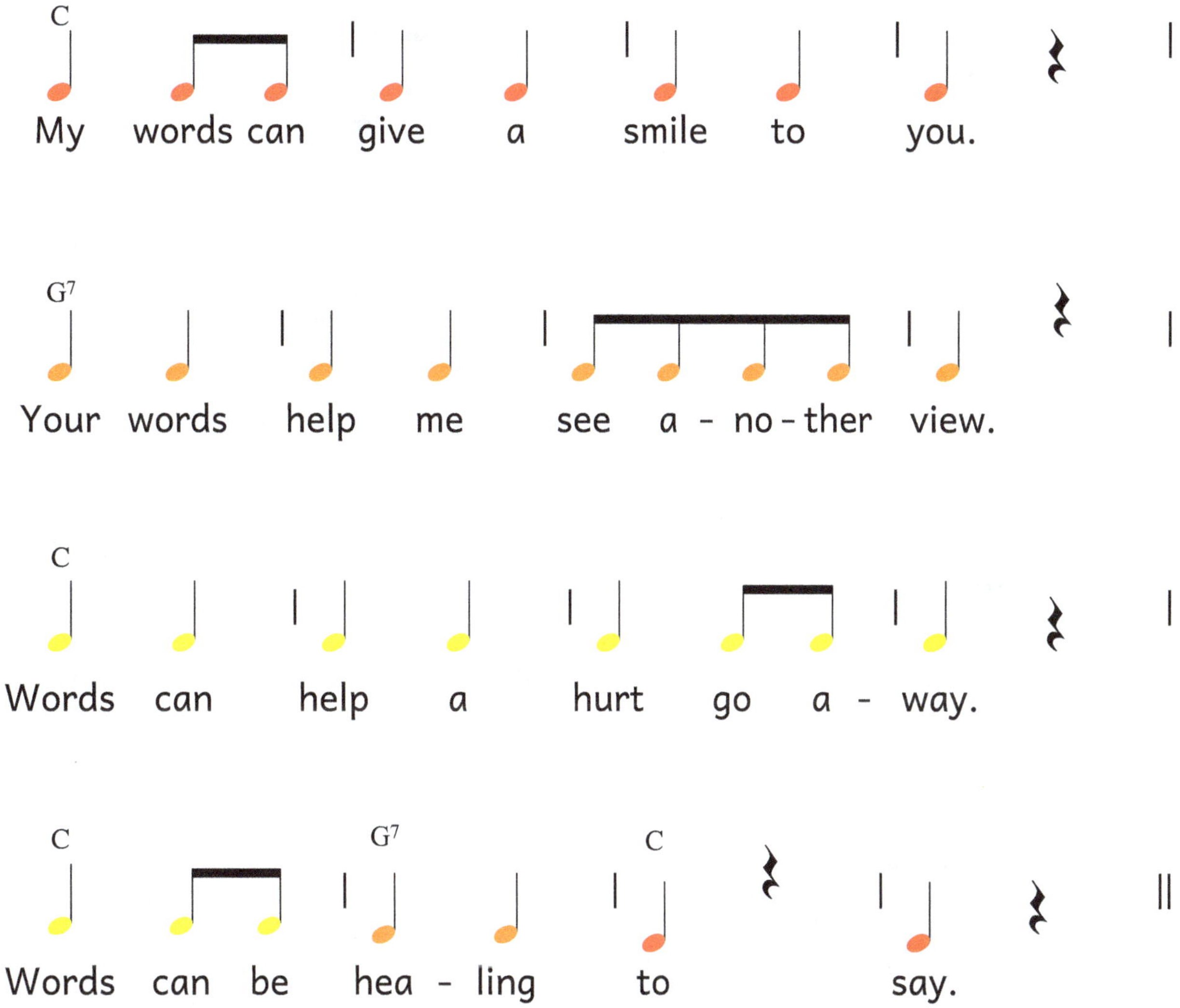

My words can give a smile to you.

Your words help me see a - no - ther view.

Words can help a hurt go a - way.

Words can be hea - ling to say.

International Phonetic Alphabet
mɪ wɜrdz kæn gɪv ə smaɪl tu ju
jʊr wɜrdz hɛlp mi si əˈnəðər vju:
wɜrdz kæn hɛlp ə hɜrt goʊ əˈweɪ
wɜrdz kæn bi ˈhilɪŋ tu seɪ

Copyright © 2024 Sarah Samuelson Studio

Español
Las palabras tienen poder curativo

Music: Sarah Samuelson

Mis pa-la-bra pue-den ha-cer-te son-re-ir.

Tus pa-la-bras am-plí-an mi per-spek-ti-va

Cuan-do ha-blas el do-lor se sien-te me-jor.

Las pa-la-bras tie-nen po-der cu-ra-ti-vo.

Español	International Phonetic Alphabet
Mis palabras pueden hacerte sonreír.	mis paˈlabras peˈðen aserˈte sonˈreir
Tus palabras amplían mi perspectiva.	tus paˈlabras amˈpljan mi perspekˈtiba
Cuando hablas, el dolor se siente mejor.	ˈkwando ˈablas, el doˈlor se ˈsjente meˈxor
Las palabras tienen poder curativo.	las paˈlabras ˈtjenen poˈðer kuraˈtivo

Copyright © 2024 Sarah Samuelson Studio

Lesson 6: harmony
Welcome Here!
Music: English Round (Hot Cross Buns)

This tune is a "round" which can be sung by two, three or four different people. The first person starts singing and when they get to the number 2, the second person starts and the same for the third and fourth person.

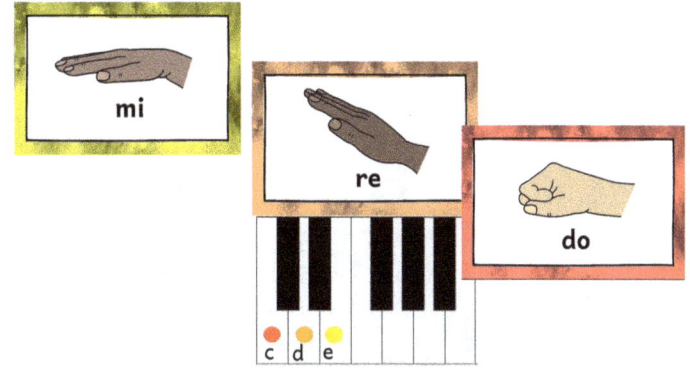

Copyright © 2024 Sarah Samuelson Studio

Español
Bienvenido aquí

Music: English Round (Hot Cross Buns)

19

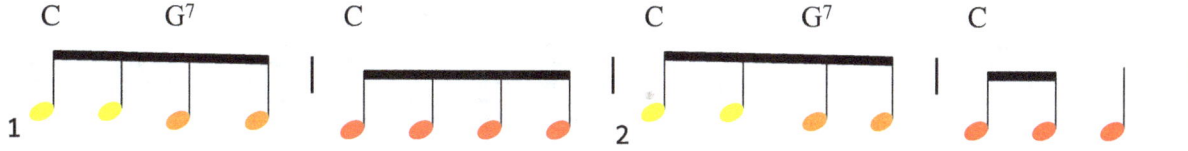

ke - ˈre mos ke   ˈto-ðos se sjen - ˈtan bjen - ˈbe - ni ðos a - ˈki
Que-re-mos que   to-dos se sien-tan bien-ven-i - dos a-quí

βa - lor - ˈa -mos   ˈla kul-ˈtu - ra   de ˈka-ða per - ˈso-na a - ˈki
Va-lor-a-mos   la cul-tu-ra   de ca-da per - so-na a-quí

Español	International Phonetic Alphabet
Queremos que todos se sientan bienvenidos aquí Valoramos la cultura de cada persona aquí	keˈremos ke ˈtoðos se ˈsjentan bjenˈbenidos aˈki ba.loˈra.mos la kulˈtu.ra de ˈka.ða perˈso.na aˈki

Copyright © 2024 Sarah Samuelson Studio

Lesson 7: 5-line staff
I Can Be a Friend
Music: France (Au Clair de la Lune)

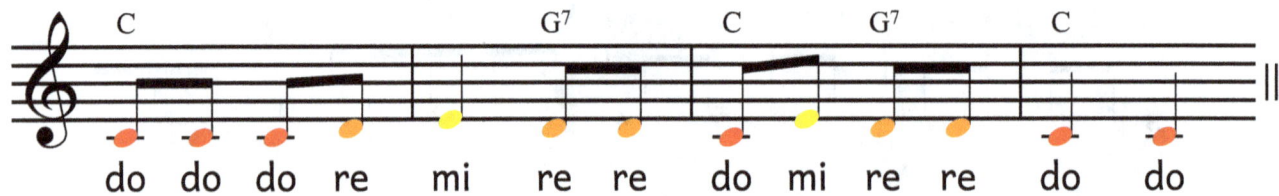

Notice that "do" which here is middle C, has a line through it to remind you that it is middle C. Can you find all of the middle Cs?

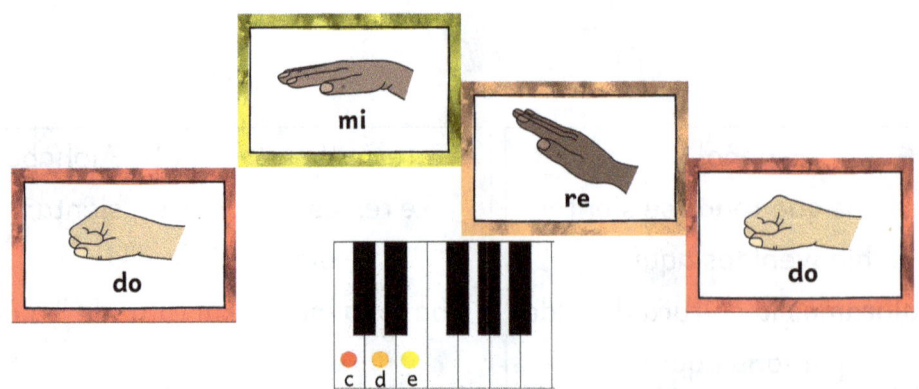

Copyright © 2024 Sarah Samuelson Studio

English
I Can Be a Friend
Music: France (Au Clair de la Lune)

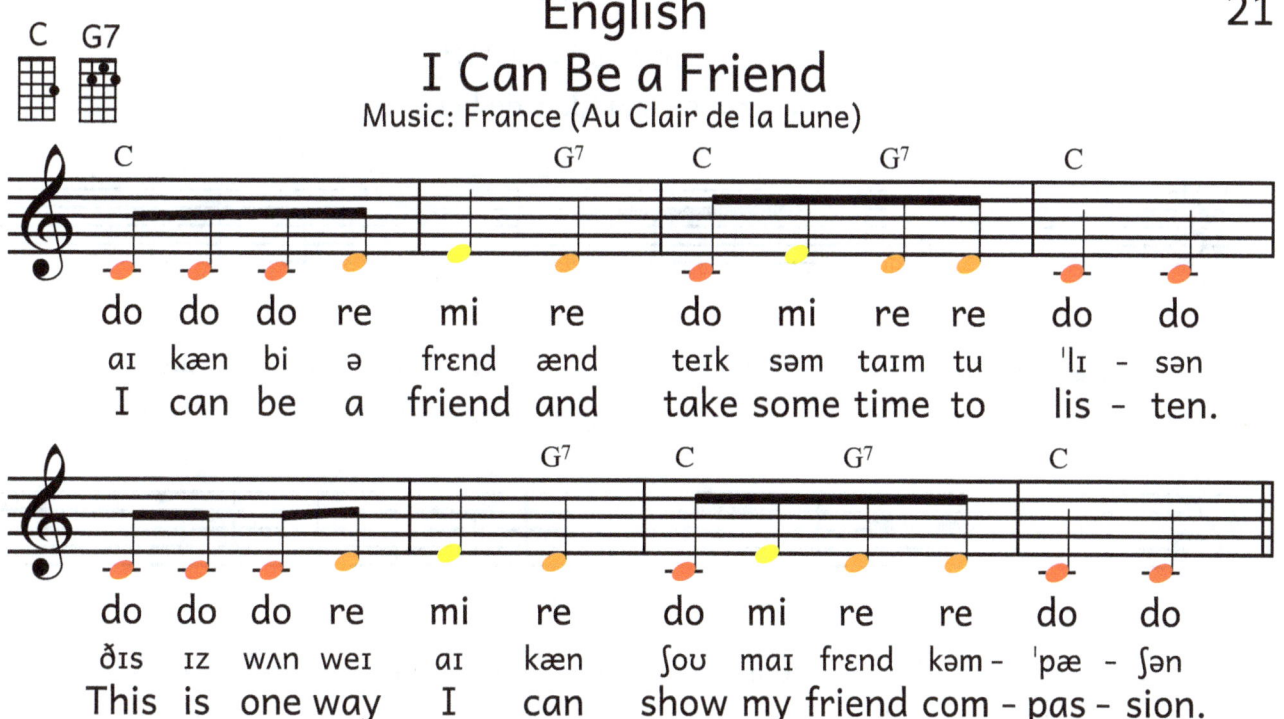

do do do re mi re do mi re re do do
aɪ kæn bi ə frɛnd ænd teɪk səm taɪm tu ˈlɪ - sən
I can be a friend and take some time to lis - ten.

do do do re mi re do mi re re do do
ðɪs ɪz wʌn weɪ aɪ kæn ʃoʊ maɪ frɛnd kəm - ˈpæ - ʃən
This is one way I can show my friend com - pas - sion.

Traditional French:	English Version:
o klɛr də la ly nə mõ na mi pjɛ ro	In the moonlight my friend Pierrot,
Au clair de la lune mon ami Pierrot	
prɛ tə mwa ta ply mə pu re kri rœ̃ mo	lend me your pen to write a word.
Prête moi ta plume pour écrire un mot.	

Copyright © 2024 Sarah Samuelson Studio

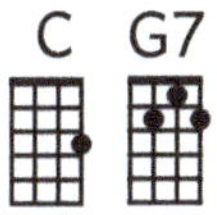

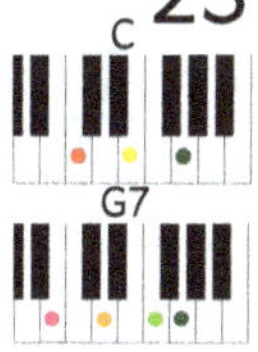

Lesson 8: do-mi
Leap for Joy
Music: Folk Song (Hop Old Squirrel)

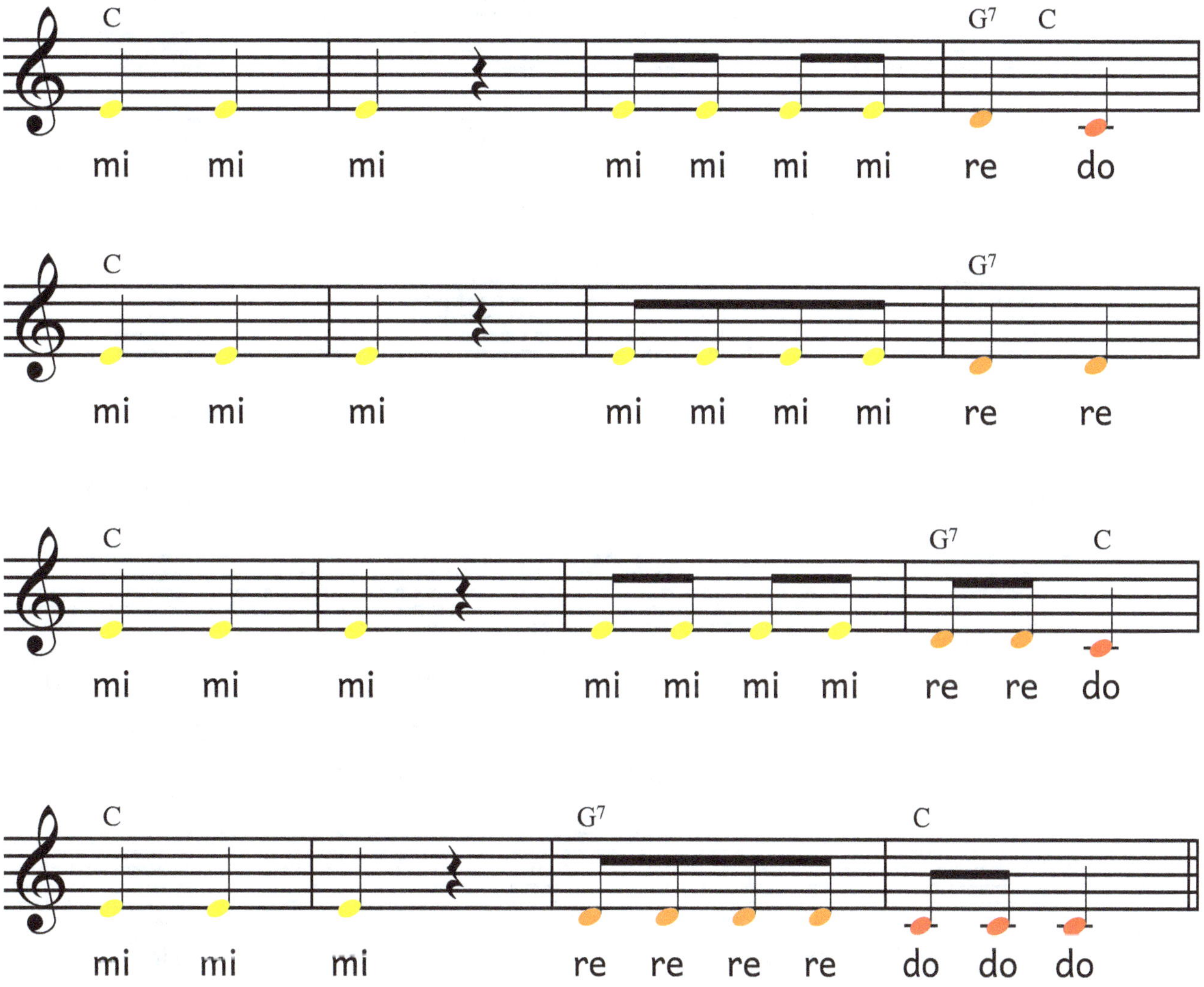

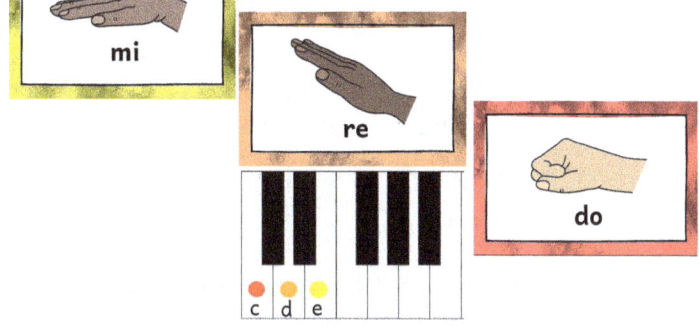

Copyright © 2024 Sarah Samuelson Studio

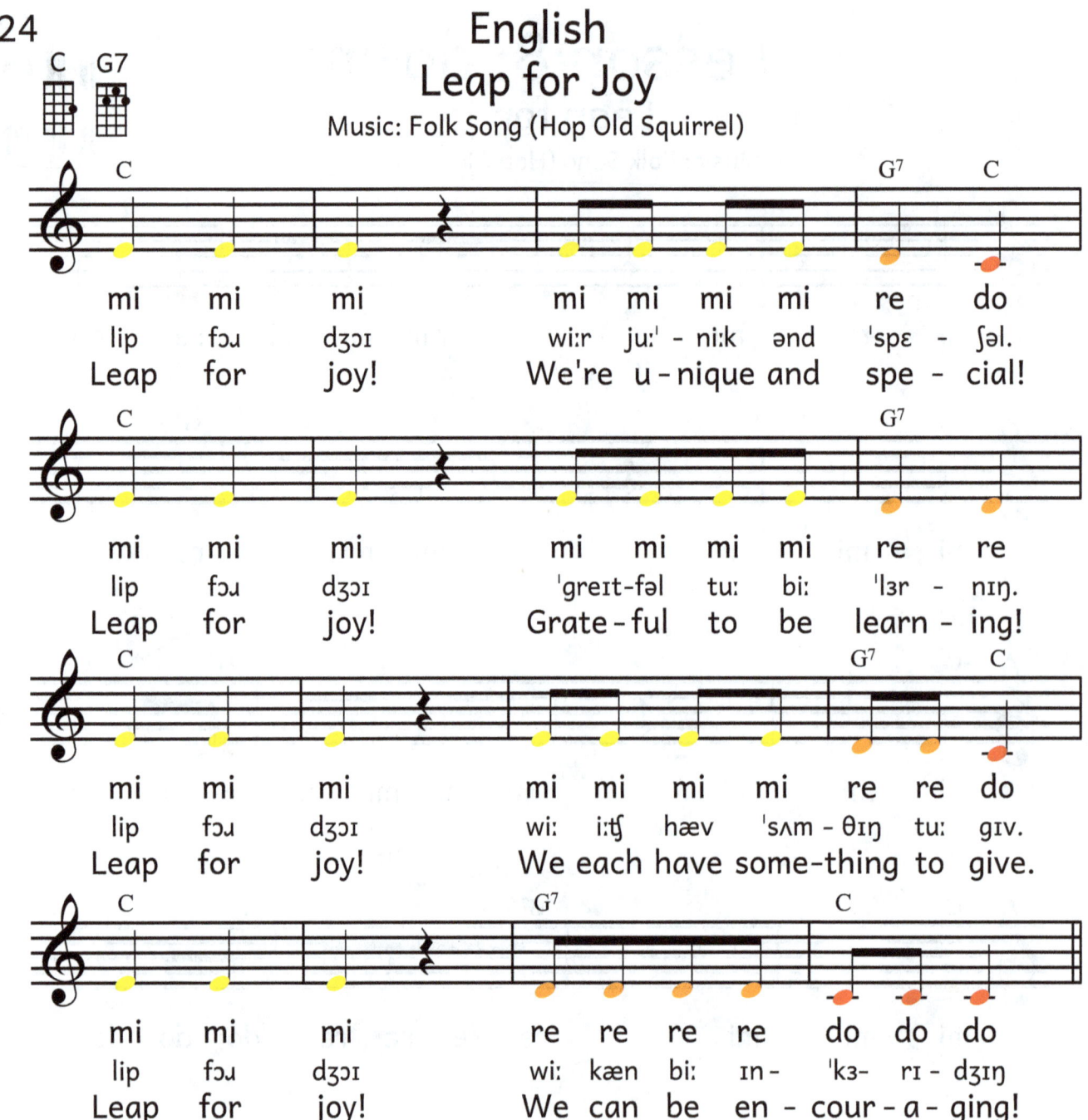

Español
Salter de alegría

Music: Folk Song (Hop Old Squirrel)

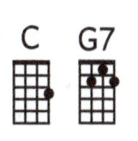

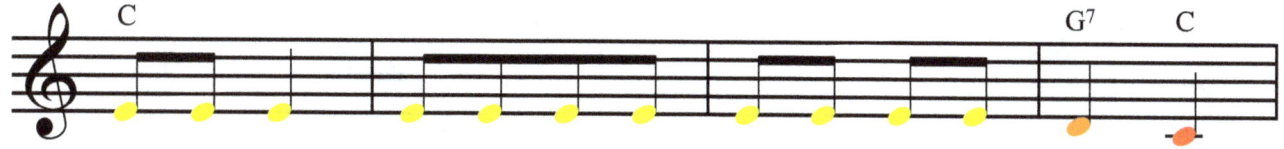

'sal - tar de   a - le - 'gri - a   'so mos es - pe - 'sja - les
Sal ter de   a - le - grí - a   So-mos es - pe - cia - les.

'sal tar de   a - le - 'gri - a   gra - sjas por   a - pren - 'der
Sal ter de   a - le - grí - a,   gra - cias por   a - pren - der.

'sal tar de   a - le - 'gri - a   ka - ða 'u - no ða 'al - go
Sal ter de   a - le - grí - a,   Ca - do u - no da al - go.

'sal - tar de   a - le - 'gri - a   a - ni - ma - mos
Sal ter de   a - le - grí - a,   a - ni - ma - mos

Copyright © 2024 Sarah Samuelson Studio

26

Lesson 9: do-mi
I Can Be More Understanding
Music: African American Spiritual (Babylon's Falling)

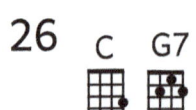
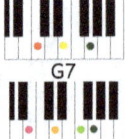
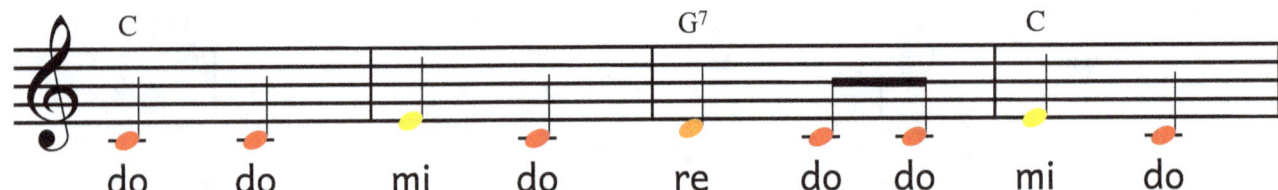
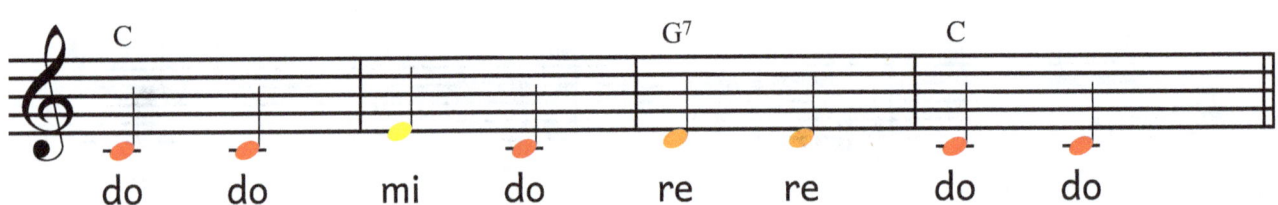

English
I Can Be More Understanding

Music: African American Spiritual (Babylon's Falling)

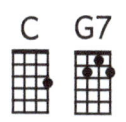

do do mi do re do do mi do
aɪ kæn lɜrn tə sɑlv ˈmɛ-ni ˈprɑ-bləmz
I can learn to solve ma-ny pro-blems.

do do mi do re re do do
aɪ kæn bi mɔr ʌn-dər-ˈstæn-dɪŋ
I can be more un-der-stand-ing

Traditional lyrics:
Babylon's falling, falling, falling,
Babylon's falling to rise no more.
Listen to: Golden Gate Quartet sing "Babylon's Falling"

Copyright © 2024 Sarah Samuelson Studio

Español
Puedo ser más comprensivo

Music: African American Spiritual (Babylon's Falling)

ˈpwe - do a - pren - ˈder a re - sol - ˈβer pro - ble - mas
Pue - do a - pren - der a re - sol - ver pro - ble - mas.

ˈpwe ðo ser mas kom - pren - ˈsi - βo
Pue do ser más com - pren - si - vo(a)

Lesson 10: do-re-mi + so
Put Yourself in Their Shoes

Text: Danielle Coke Balfour; Music: Spiritual (Oh, I'm Goin' to Sing)

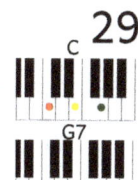

so mi mi mi mi re re re re do do do

re re re re mi mi so mi re do

> Treble clef is also called G Clef and shows where G is on the 5-line staff. This G is "so."
> Notice the curly part of the clef looks like a G.

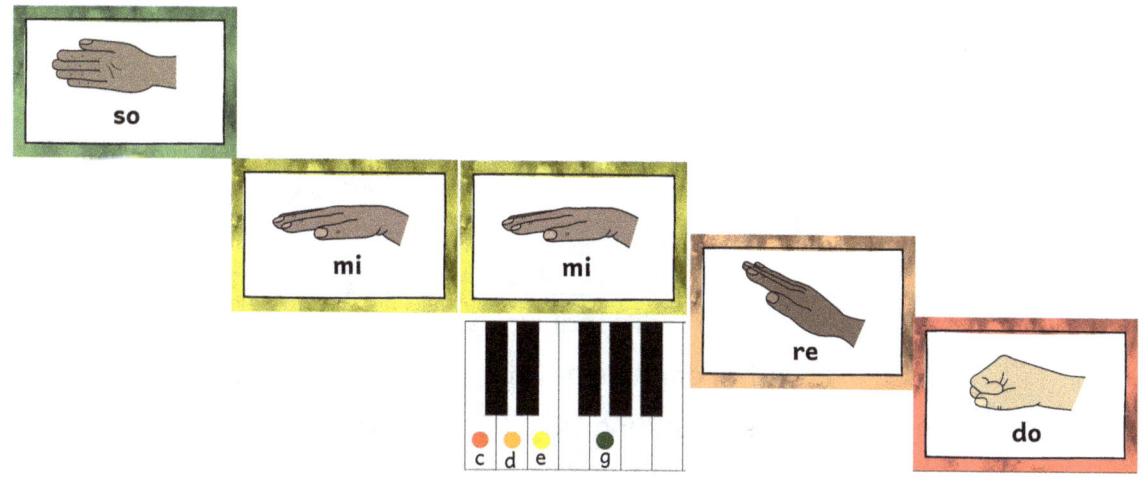

English
Put Yourself in Their Shoes

Text: Danielle Coke Balfour; Music: Spiritual (Oh, I'm Gonna Sing)

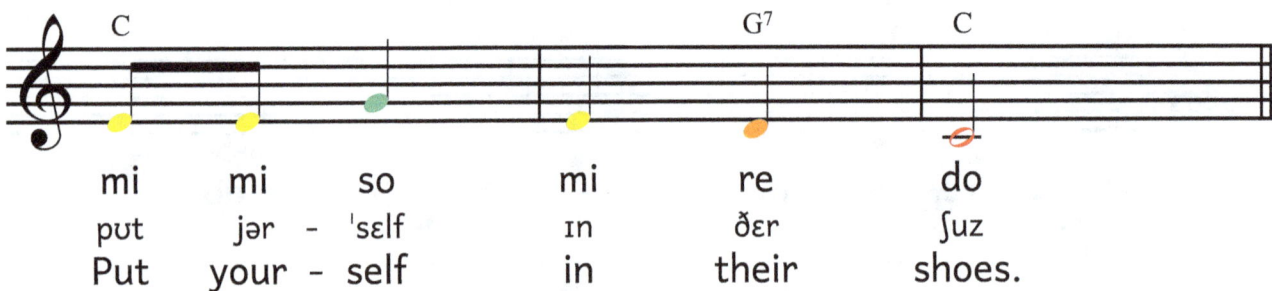

Traditional lyrics:
Oh I'm gonna sing, gonna sing,
gonna sing, gonna sing along my way.

Copyright © 2024 Sarah Samuelson Studio

Español
Ponte en su Lugar

Music: African American Spiritual (Oh, I'm Gonna Sing)

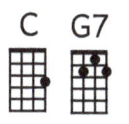

ˈno de-βe-ˈri-a su-θer-ˈder-te pa-ra im-por ˈtar - te
"No de-be-rí-a su-ce-der-te pa-ra im-por-tar-te

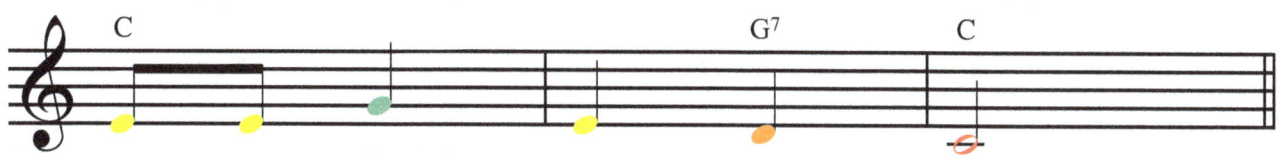

ˈpon - te en su lu - ˈɣar
Pon - te en su lu - gar.

Copyright © 2024 Sarah Samuelson Studio

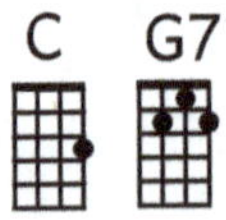

Lesson 11: so & half note
We Want All to Feel Connected
Music: USA (Mary Had a Little Lamb)

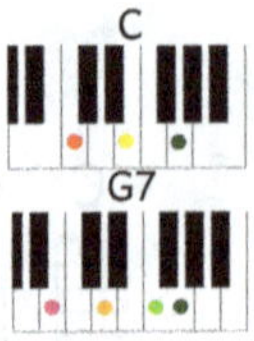

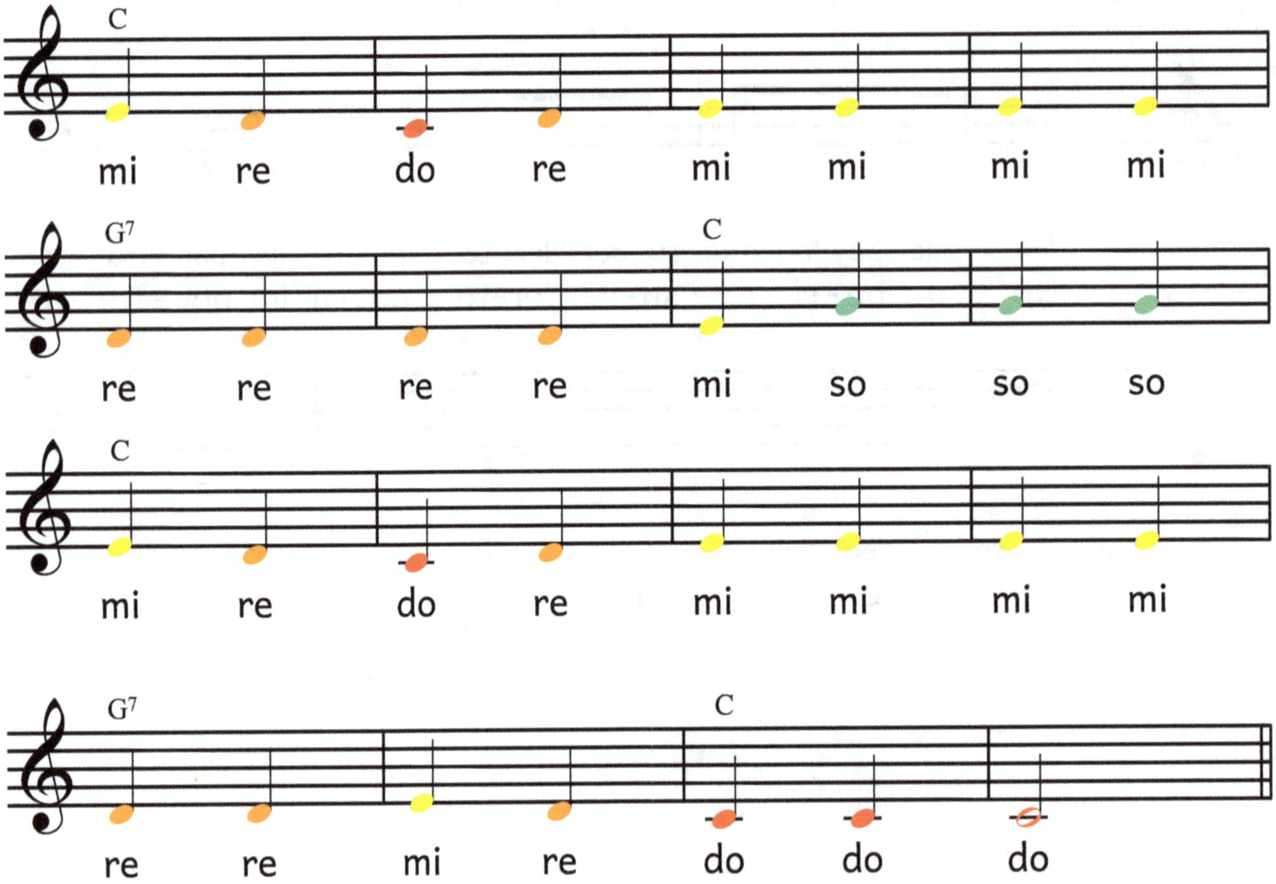

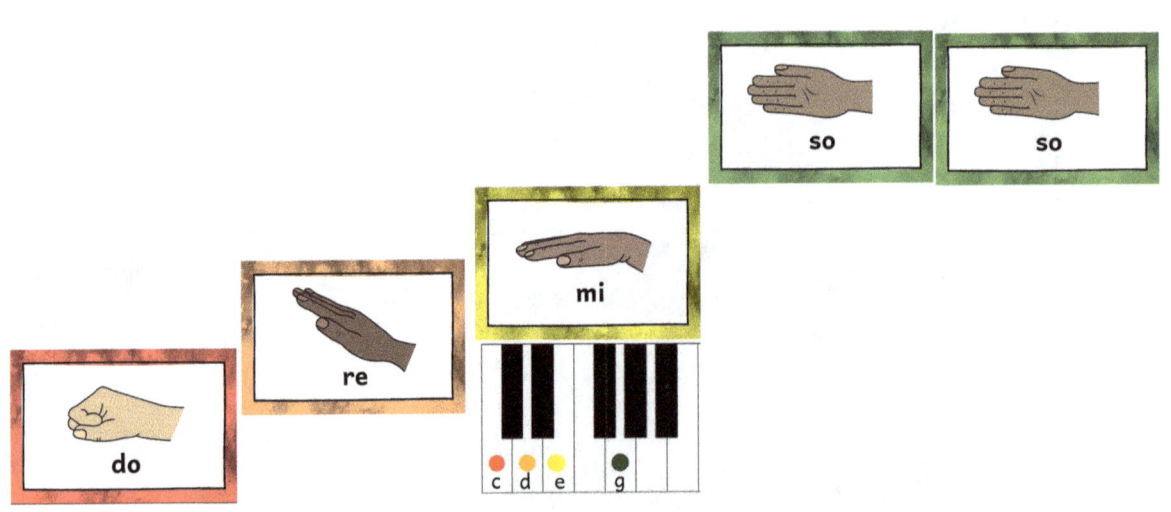

English
We Want All to Feel Connected

Music: USA (Mary Had a Little Lamb)

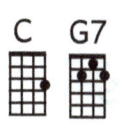

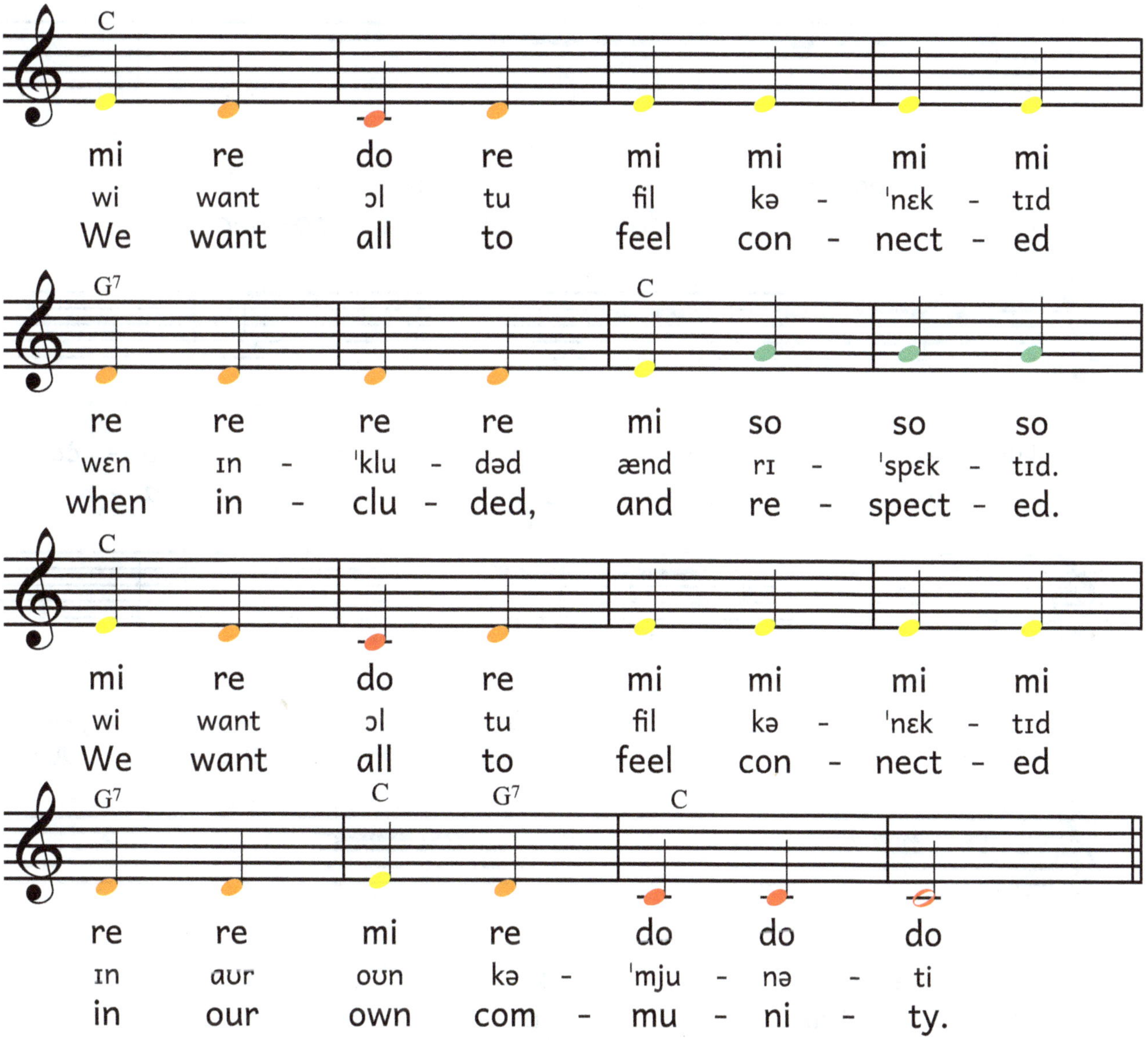

mi re do re mi mi mi mi
wi want ɔl tu fil kə-ˈnɛk-tɪd
We want all to feel con-nect-ed

re re re re mi so so so
wɛn ɪn-ˈklu-dəd ænd rɪ-ˈspɛk-tɪd.
when in-clu-ded, and re-spect-ed.

mi re do re mi mi mi mi
wi want ɔl tu fil kə-ˈnɛk-tɪd
We want all to feel con-nect-ed

re re mi re do do do
ɪn aʊr oʊn kə-ˈmju-nə-ti
in our own com-mu-ni-ty.

Traditional lyrics:
Mary had a little lamb, little lamb, little lamb, Mary had a little lamb it's fleece was white as snow.

Copyright © 2024 Sarah Samuelson Studio

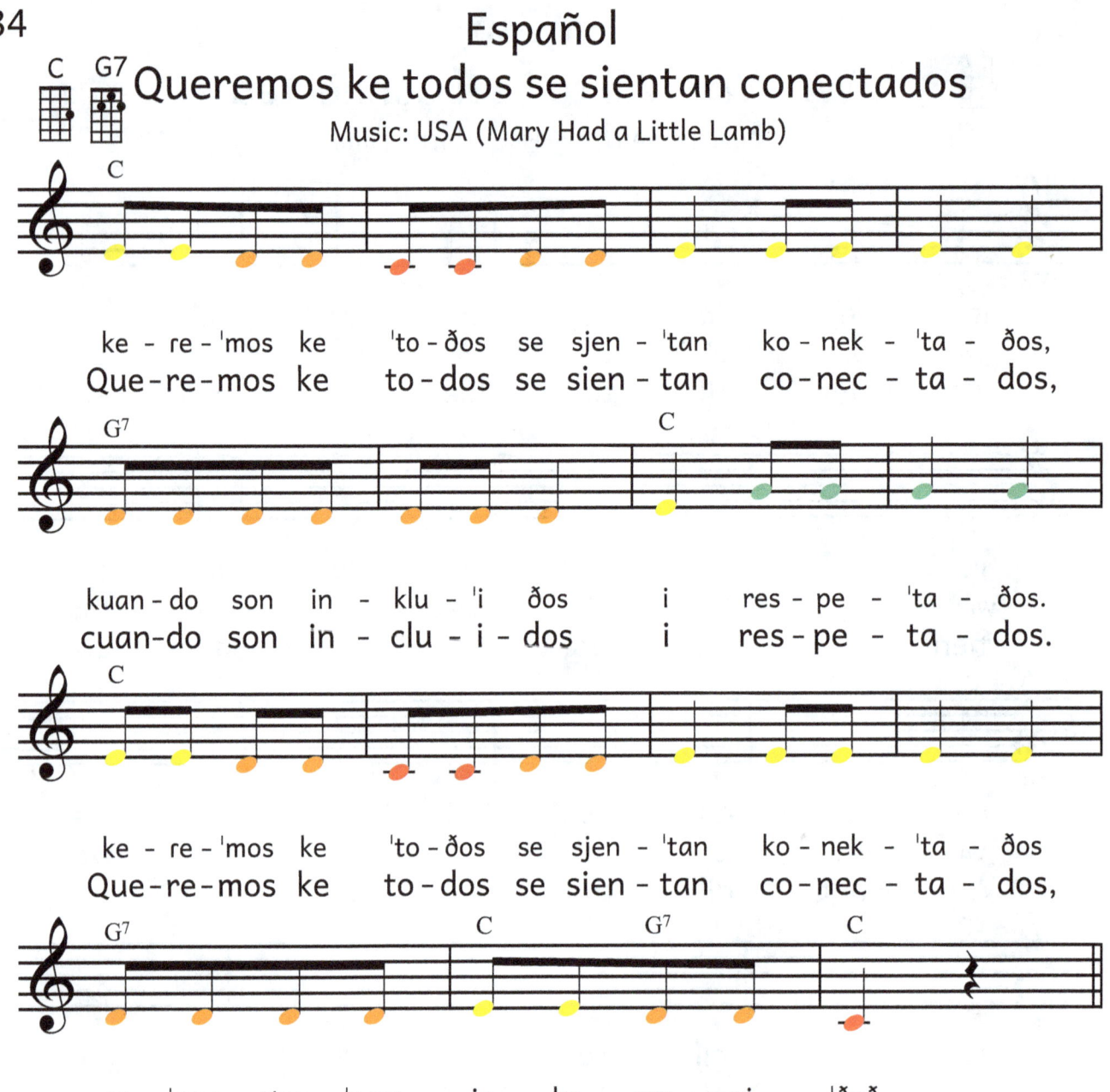

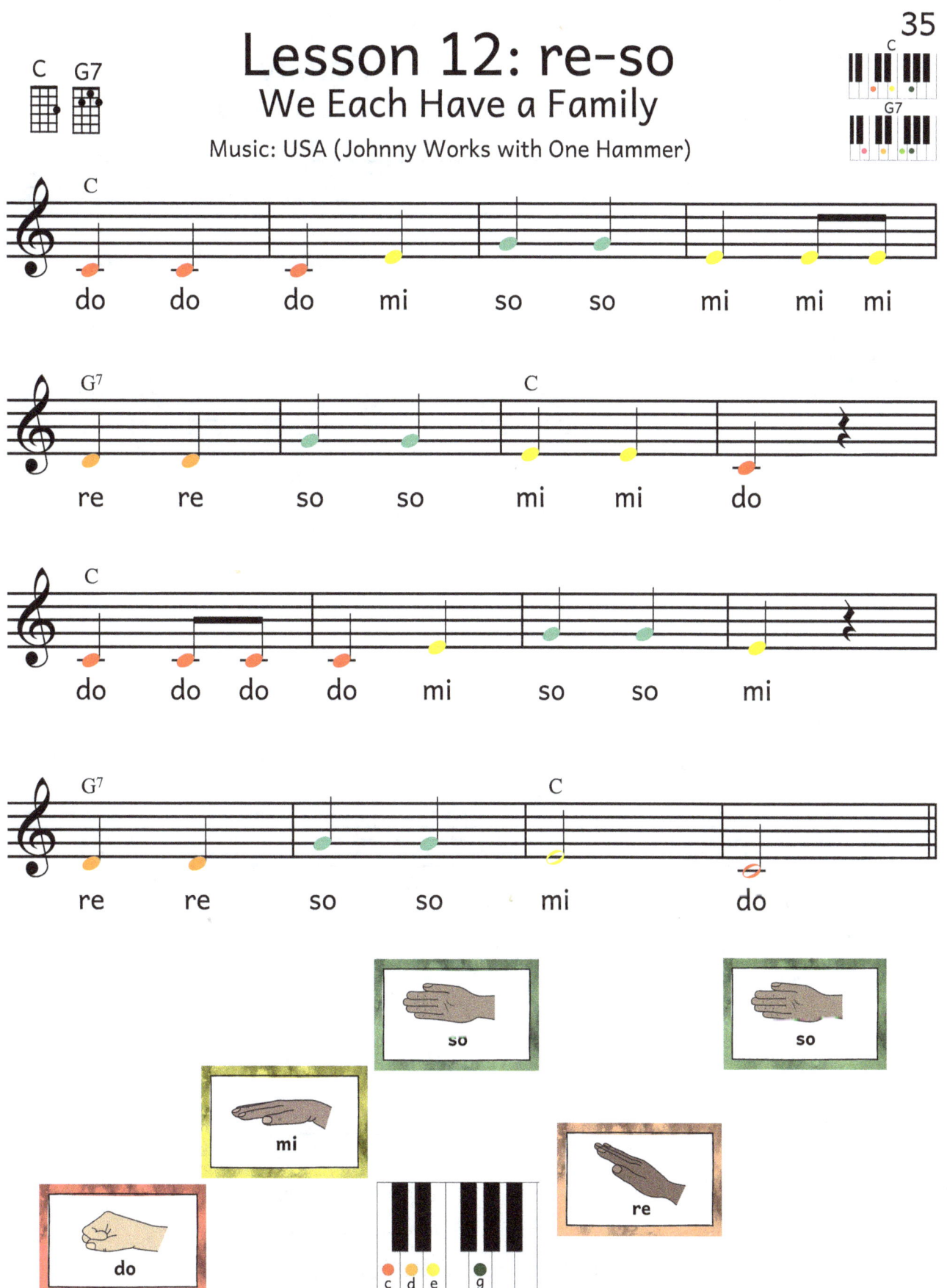

English
We Each Have a Family
Music: USA (Johnny Works with One Hammer)

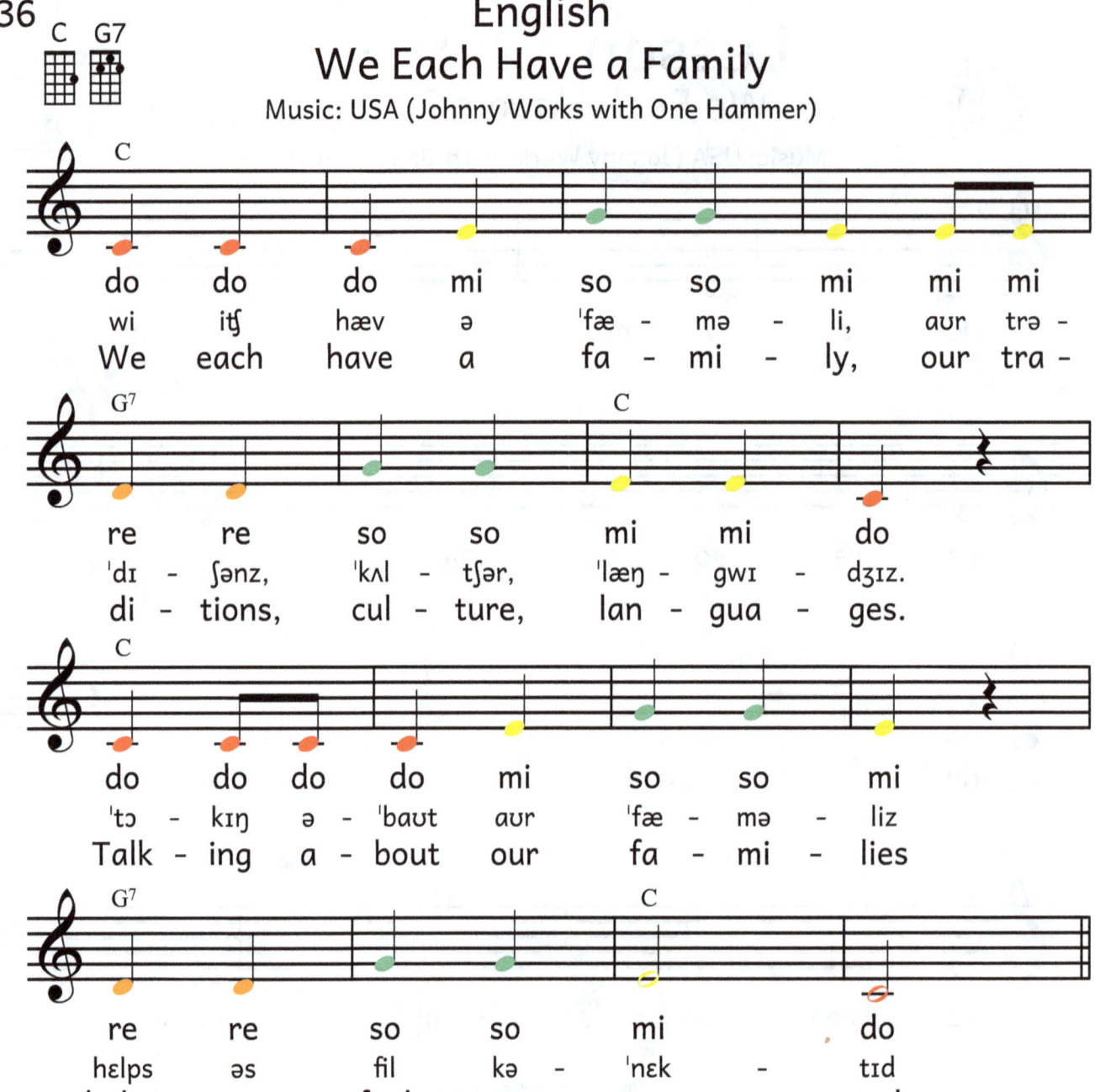

Traditional lyrics:
Johnny works with one hammer, one hammer, one hammer; Johnny works with one hammer, then he works with two.

Copyright © 2024 Sarah Samuelson Studio

Español
Cada Uno Tiene Una Familia
Music: USA (Johnny Works with One Hammer)

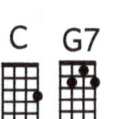

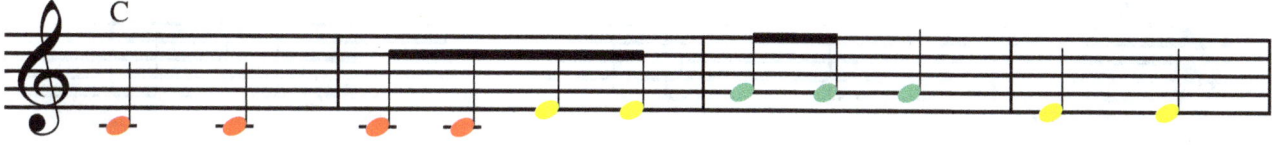

ˈka - ða   ˈu - no   tje - ne   u - na   fa - ˈmil - ja
Ca - da   u - no   tie - ne   u - na   fa - mil - ia,

tra - ði - ˈsjo - nes, kul - ˈtu - ra, i - ˈdjo - mas.
tra - di - cio - nes, cul - tu - ra, i - dio - mas.

ˈa - blar de   ˈnues - tras fa - ˈmil - jas nos a - ˈju - da
Ha - blar de   nue - stras fa - mi - lias nos a - yu - da

a sen - ˈtir - nos ko - nek - ˈta - dos
a sen tir - nos co - nec - ta - dos.

Copyright © 2024 Sarah Samuelson Studio

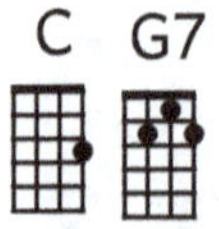

Lesson 13: so-mi
Little Changes Make a Difference
Music: Robert Lowry

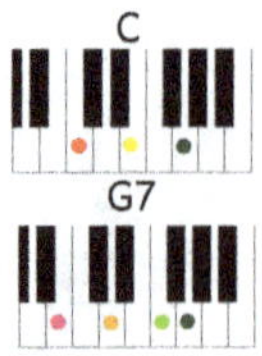

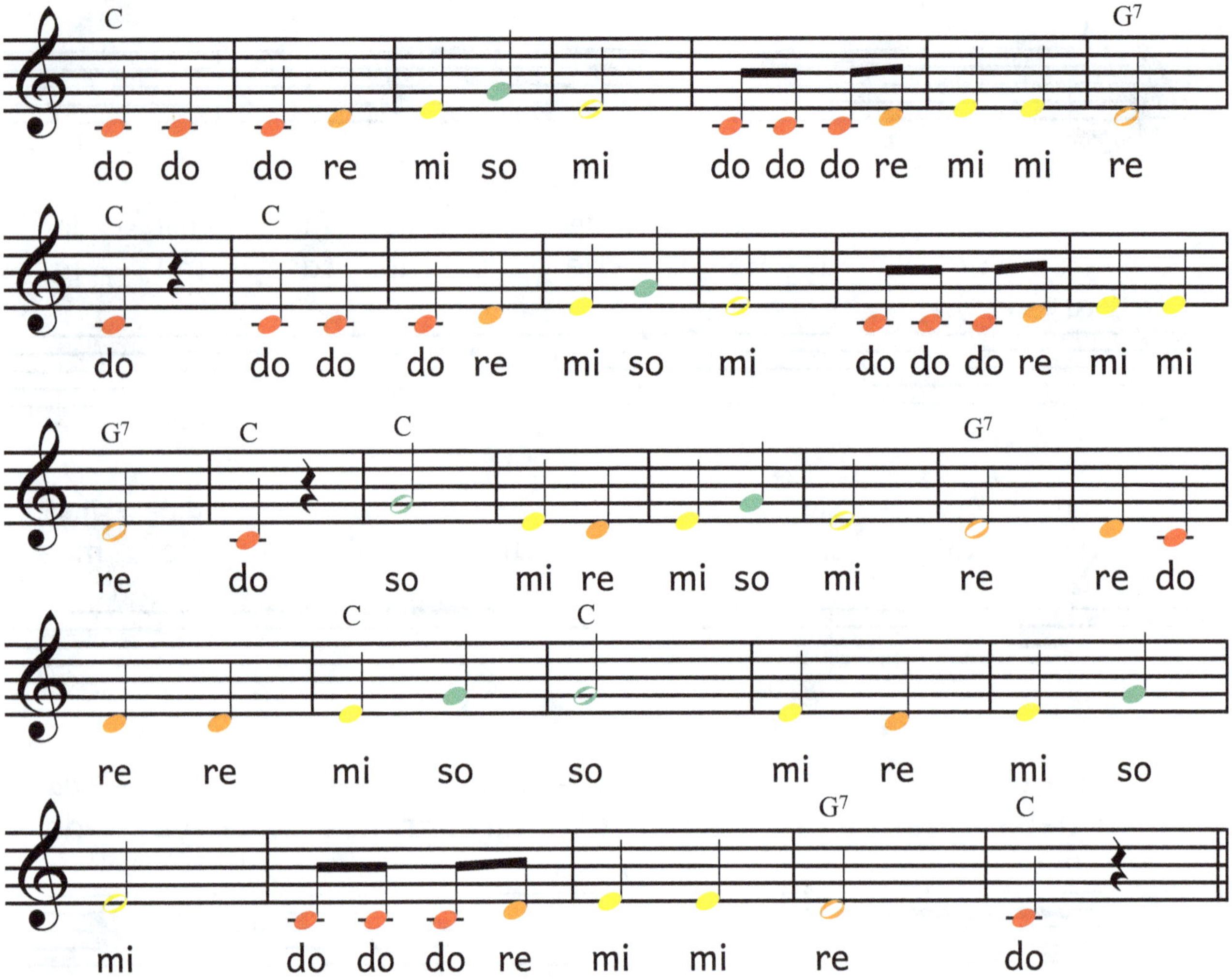

do do do re mi so mi do do do re mi mi re

do do do re mi so mi do do do re mi mi

re do so mi re mi so mi re re do

re re mi so so mi re mi so

mi do do do re mi mi re do

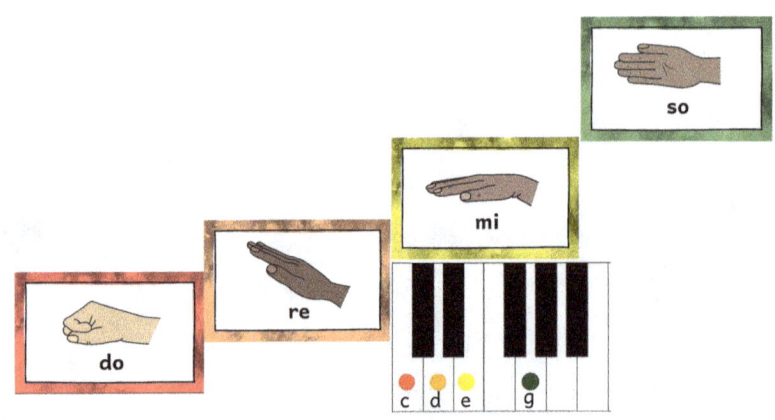

Copyright © 2024 Sarah Samuelson Studio

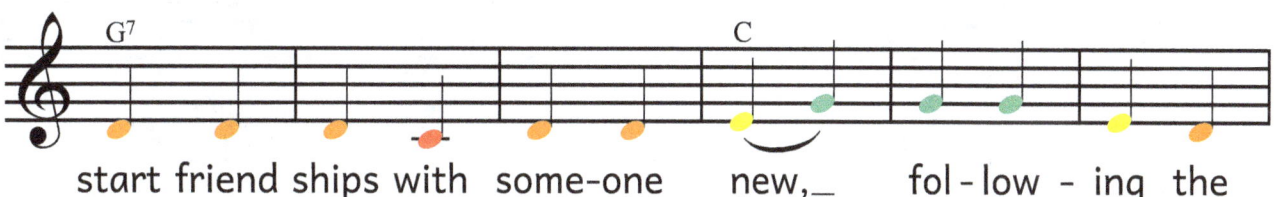

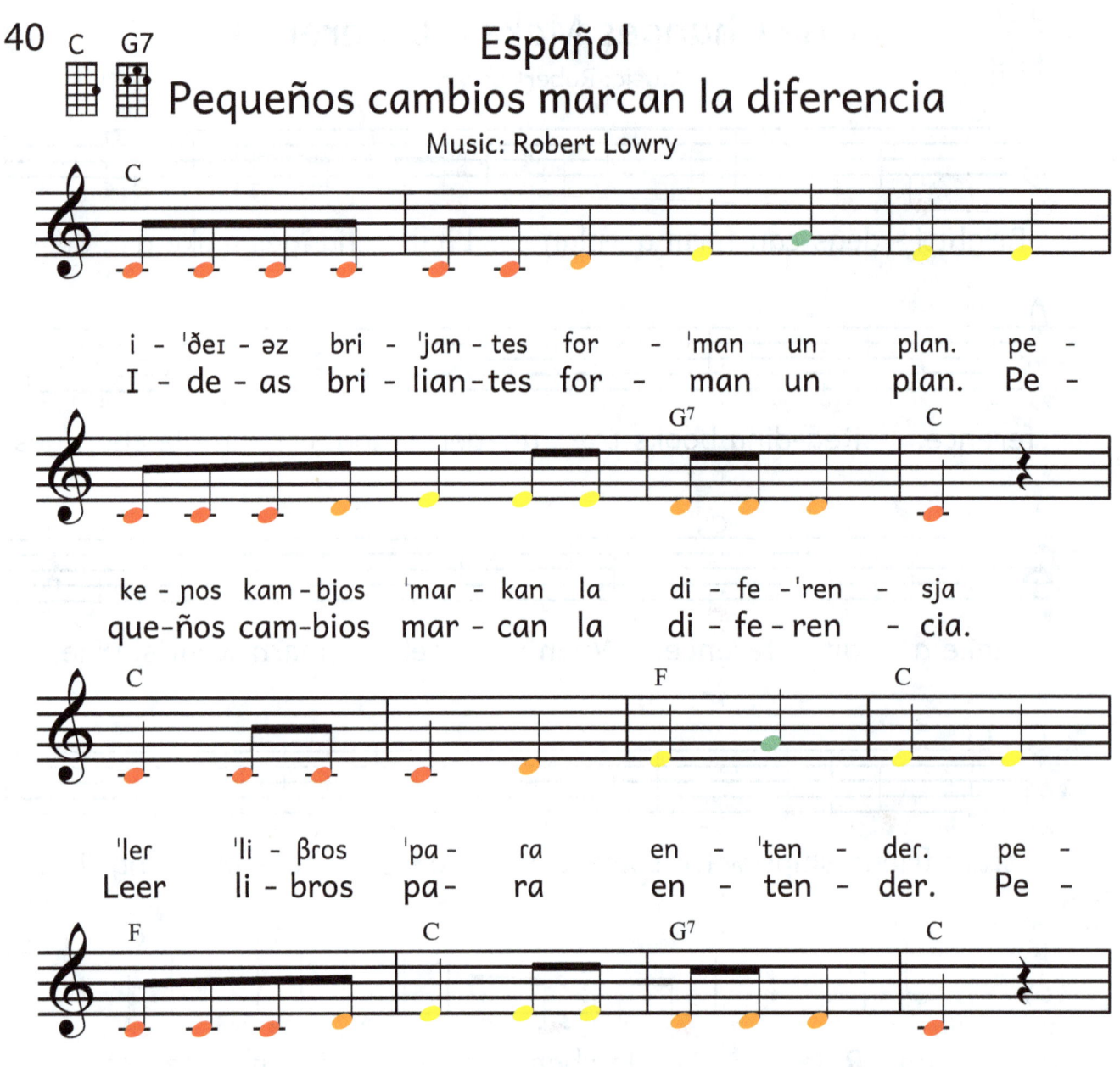

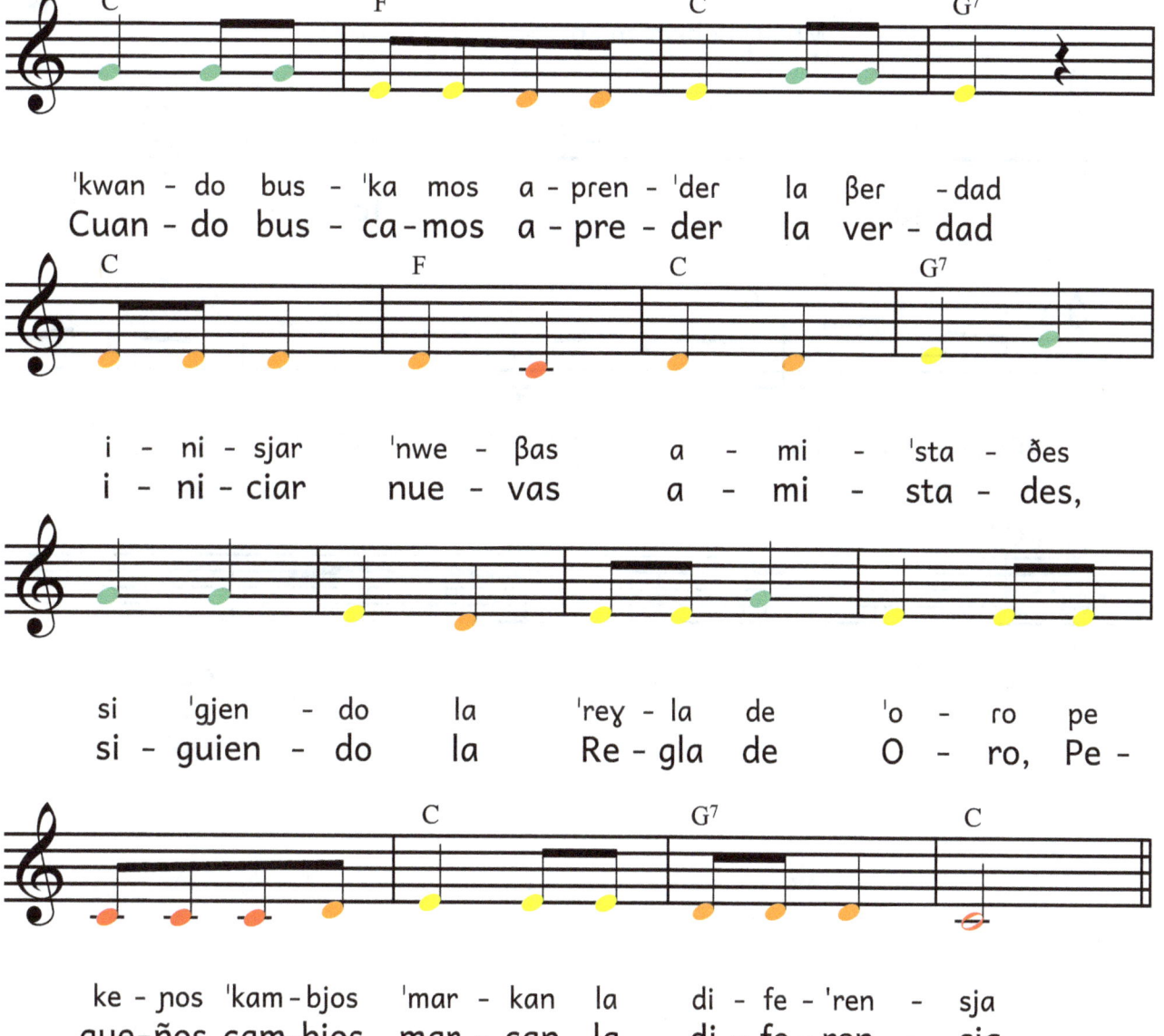

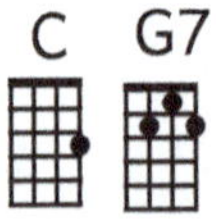

Lesson 14: fa-re
Our Voice is Important
Music: Bohemian Folk Song (Honeybee)

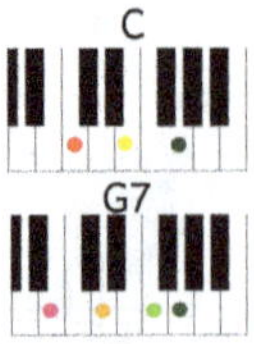

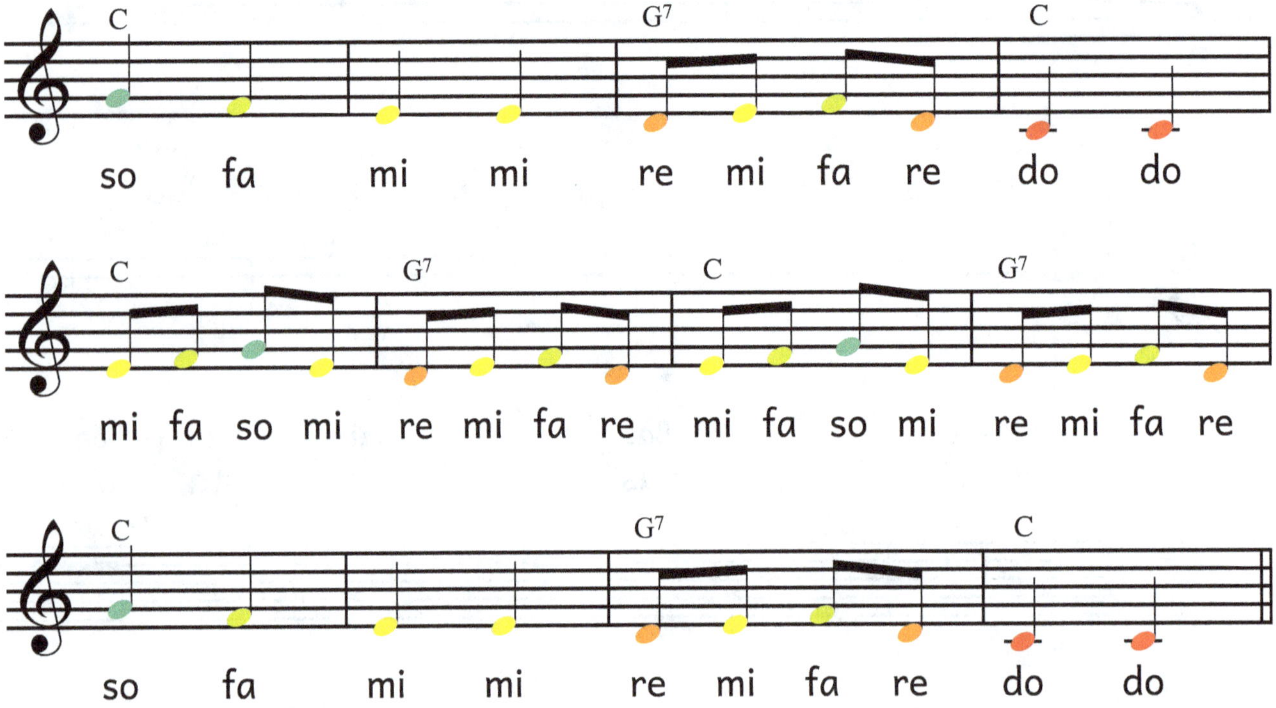

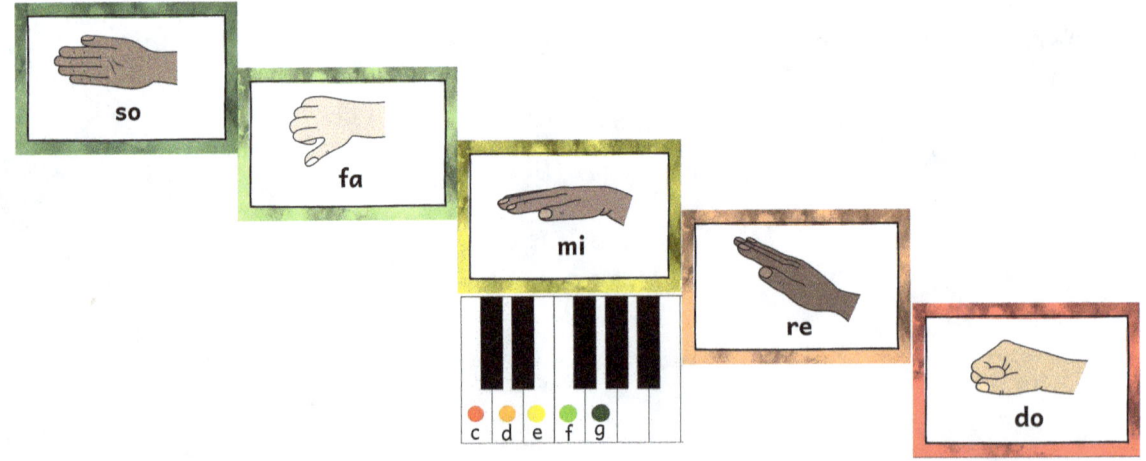

43

English
Our Voice is Important
Music: Bohemian Folk Song (Honeybee)

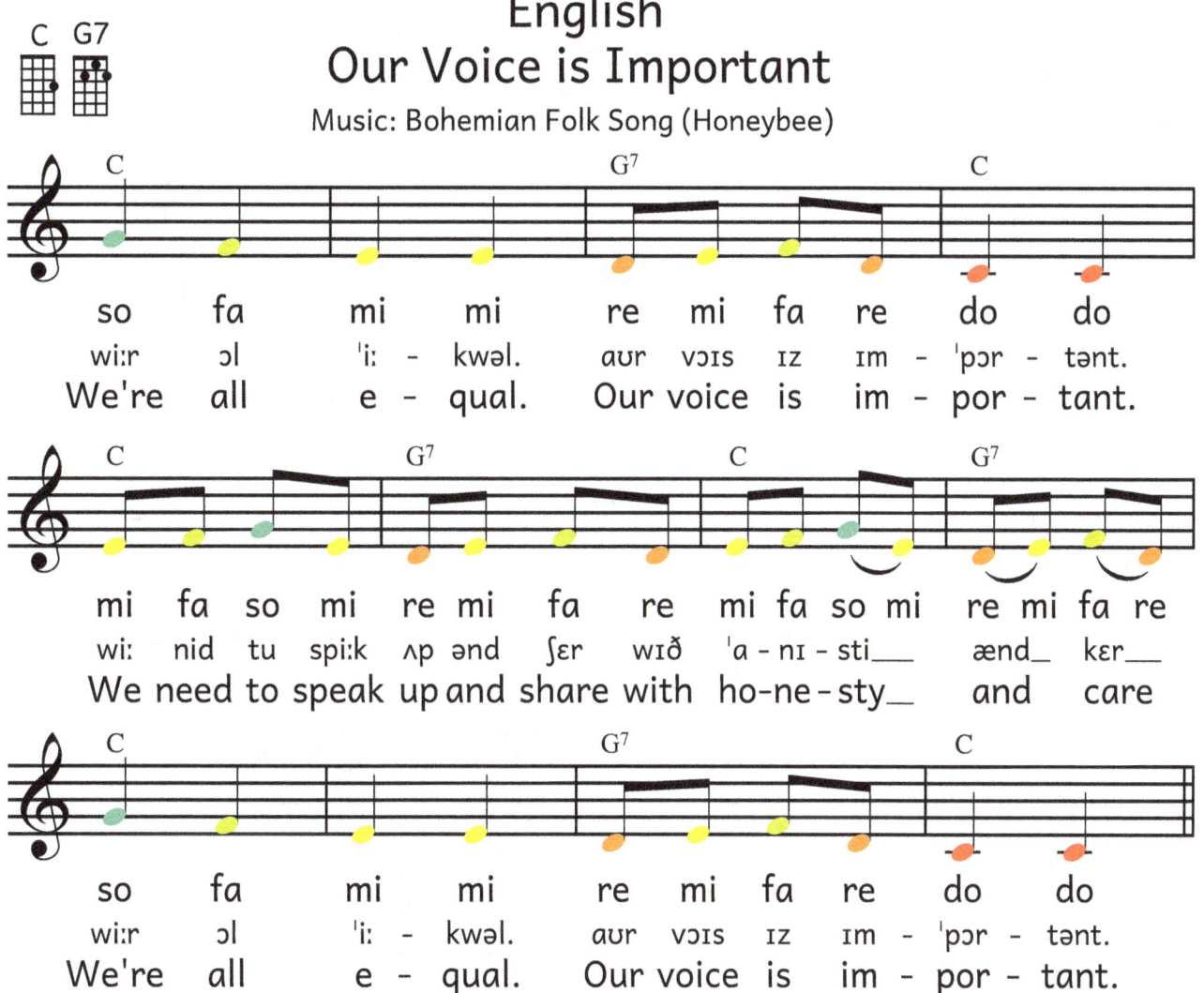

Traditional lyrics:
Honeybee, buzzing busily, Making honey from a flower hour after busy hour.
Honeybee, see the honeybee.

Copyright © 2024 Sarah Samuelson Studio

Español
Nuestra voz importa
Music: Bohemian Folk Song (Honeybee)

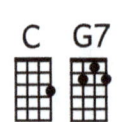

ˈto - dos ˈso - mos i - ˈgwa - les. ˈnwes - tra ˈβos im - ˈpor - ta
To - dos so - mos i - gua - les. Nue - stra voz im - por - ta.

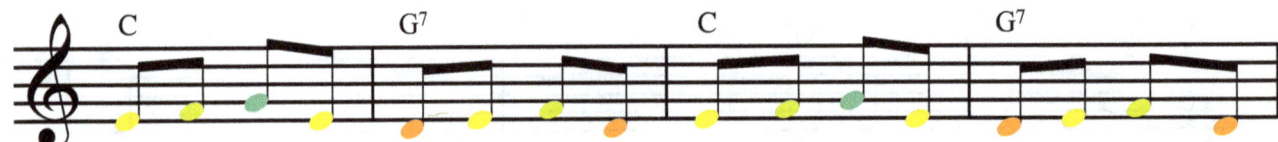

ne - se - ˈsi - ta - mos a - ˈblar i kom - par - ˈtir kon o - ne - ˈsti- dað
Ne - ce - si - ta - mos ha-blar y com-par-tir con ho-ne-sti- dad.

ˈto - dos ˈso - mos i - ˈgwa - les. ˈnwes - tra ˈβos im - ˈpor - ta
To - dos so - mos i - gua - les. Nue - stra voz im - por - ta.

Copyright © 2024 Sarah Samuelson Studio

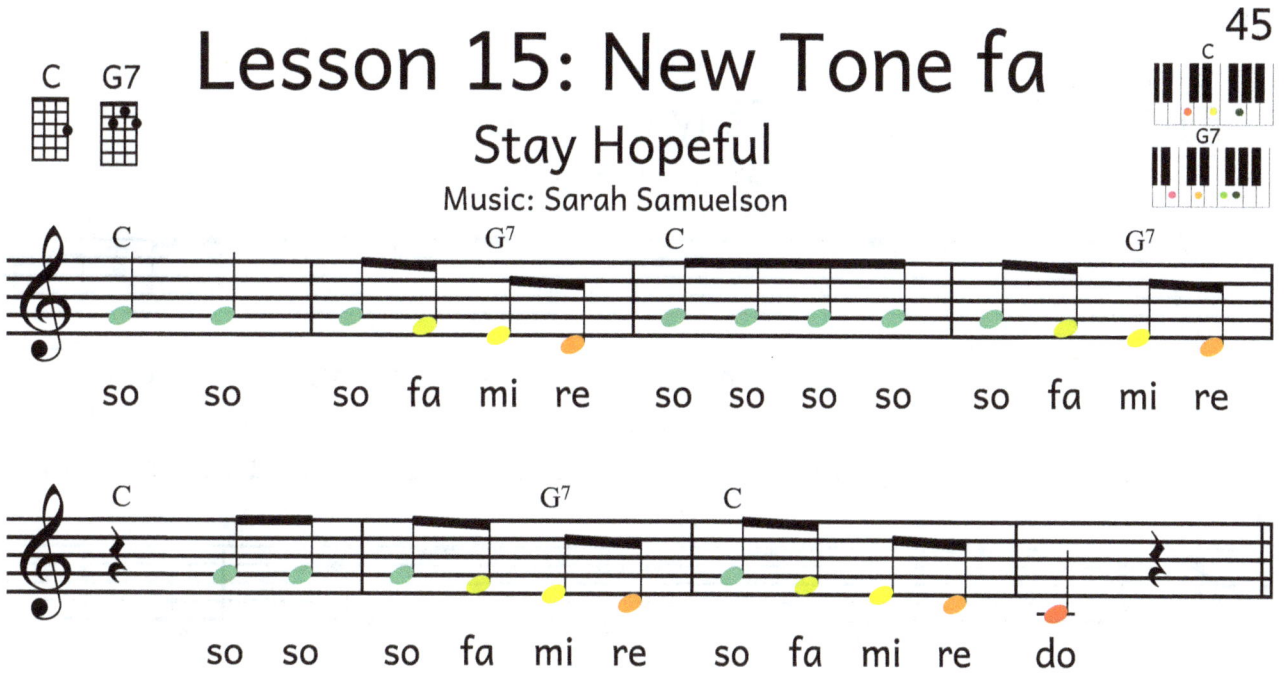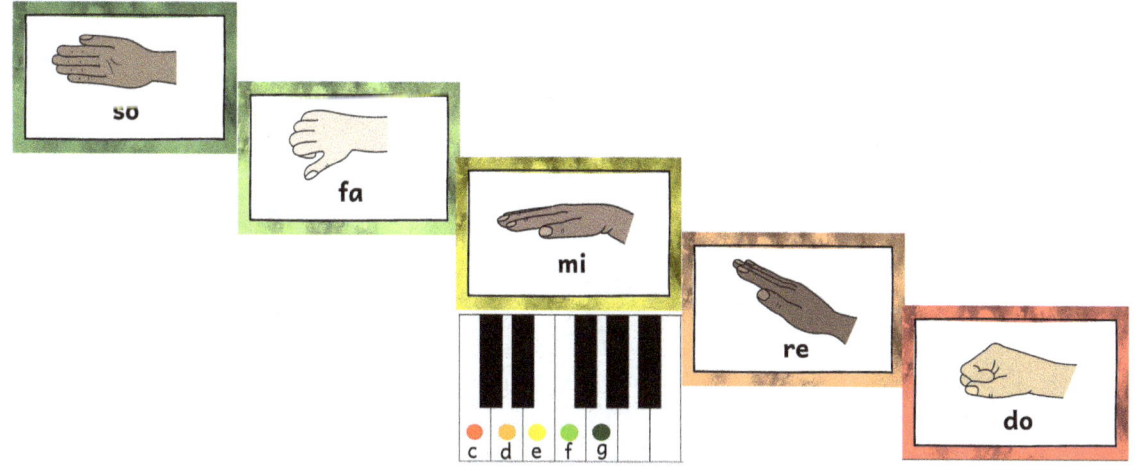

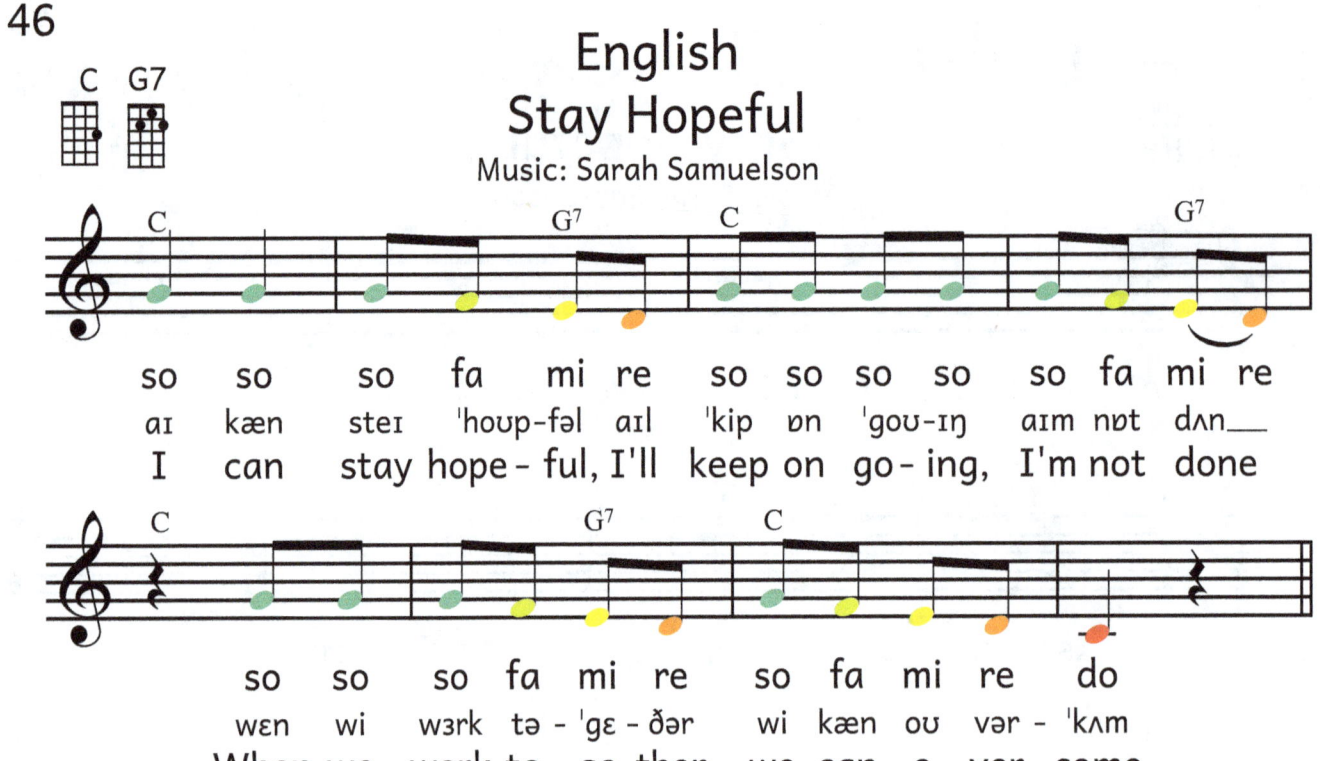

Español
Puedo tener esperanza
Music: Sarah Samuelson

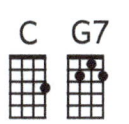

'pwe-do te-'ner es-pe-'ran-sa se-gi-'re a-ðe-'lan-te
Pue-do te-ner es-pe-ran-za; se-gui-ré a-de-lan-te

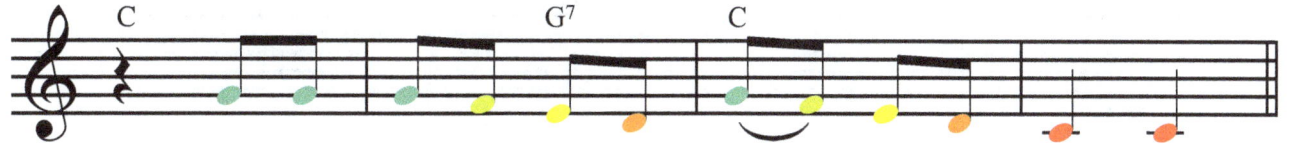

tra-βa-'xan-do 'xun-tos, lo___ su-pe-'ra-mos
Tra-ba-jan-do jun-tos lo___ su-pe-ra-mos.

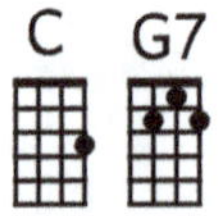

Lesson 16: so,
Care For My Neighbor
Music: Germany (Mäh, Lämmchen, Mäh)

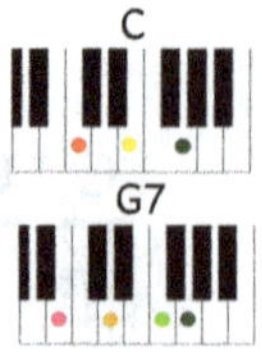

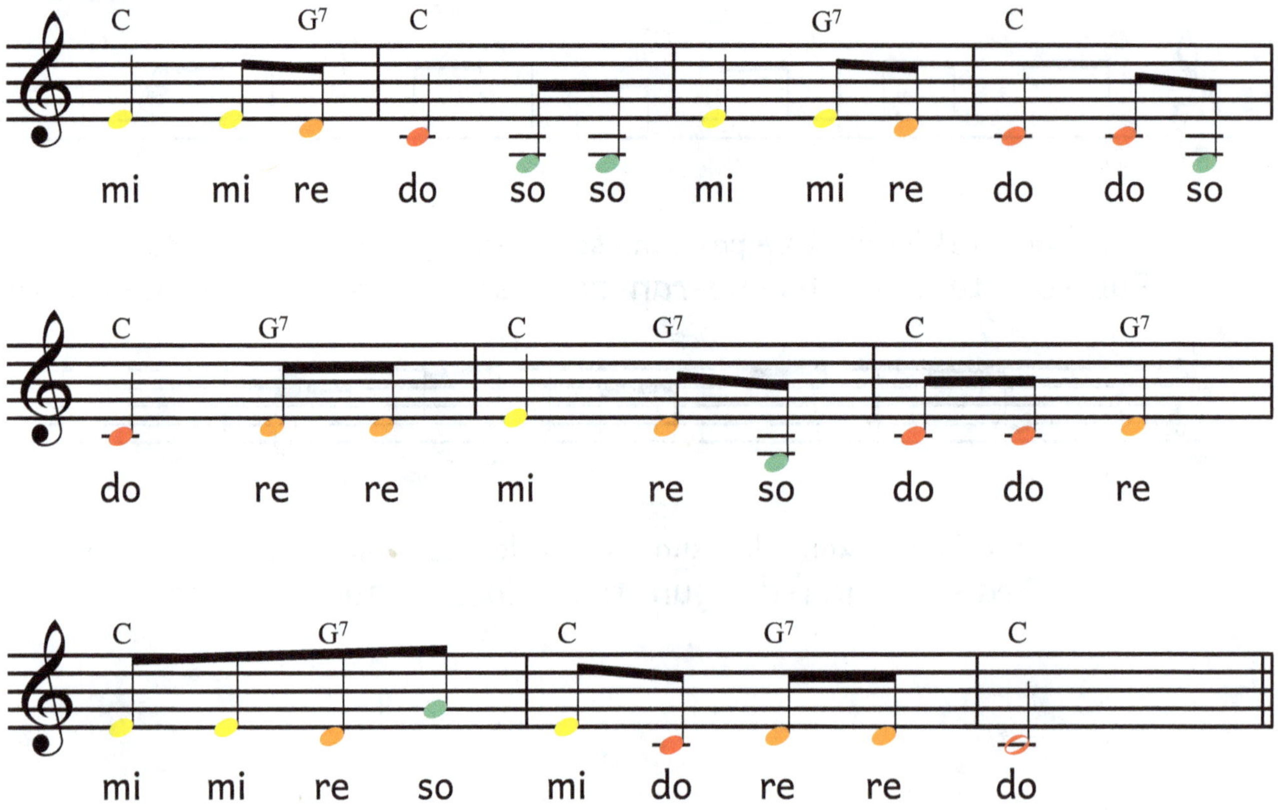

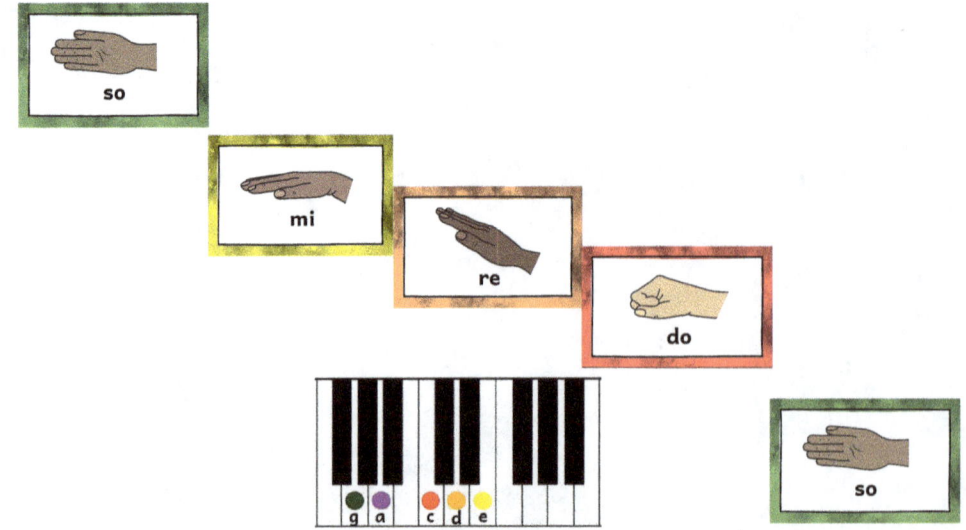

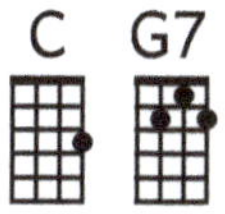
C G7

English

Care For My Neighbor

Music: Germany (Mäh, Lämmchen, Mäh)

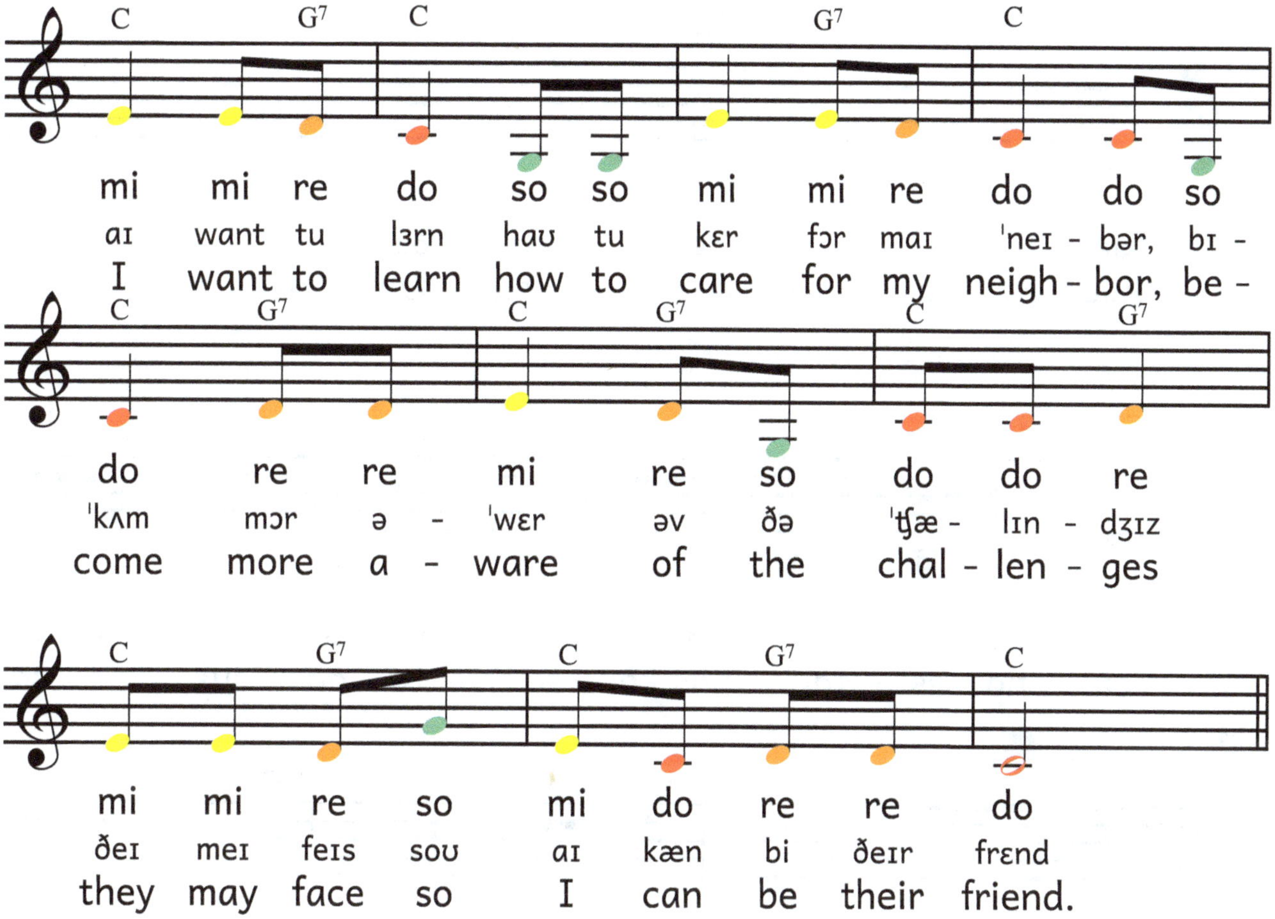
C G7 C G7 C
mi mi re do so so mi mi re do do so
aɪ want tu lɜrn haʊ tu kɛr fɔr maɪ ˈneɪ - bər, bɪ -
I want to learn how to care for my neigh - bor, be -
C G7 C G7 C G7
do re re mi re so do do re
ˈkʌm mɔr ə - ˈwɛr əv ðə ˈʧæ - lɪn - dʒɪz
come more a - ware of the chal - len - ges
C G7 C G7 C
mi mi re so mi do re re do
ðeɪ meɪ feɪs soʊ aɪ kæn bi ðeɪr frɛnd
they may face so I can be their friend.

50

Español
Cuidar a mi Vecino
Music: Germany (Mäh, Lämmchen, Mäh)

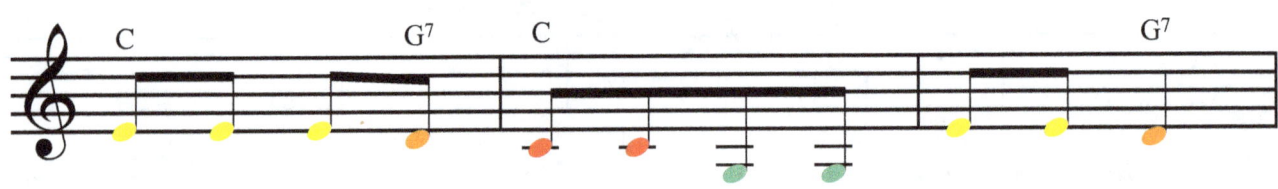

ˈkje - ro a - pren - ˈder a kwi - ˈðar a mi be -
Quie - ro a - pren - der a cui - dar a mi ve -

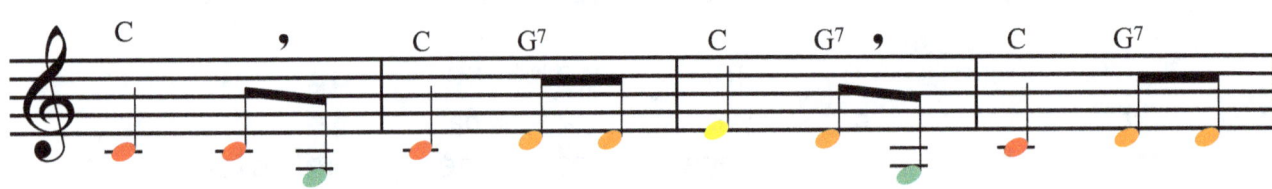

ˈsi - no, ˈes - tar mas kon - ˈsjen - te de sus de - sa -
ci - no, es - tar más kon - scien - te de sus de - sa

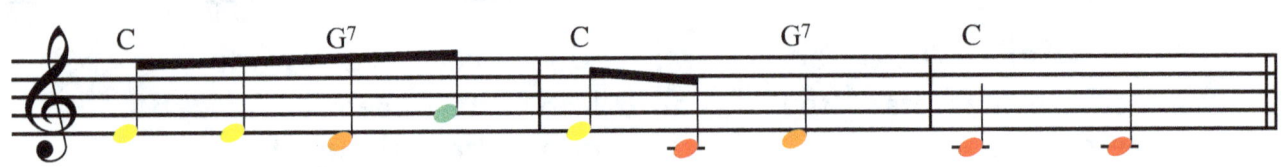

ˈfi - os pa - ra ser su a - ˈmi - go
fí - os pa - ra ser su a - mi - go.

Copyright © 2024 Sarah Samuelson Studio

Lesson 17: so, & la,
We Want Justice in Our World
Music: Spiritual (Oh! Oh! Freedom)

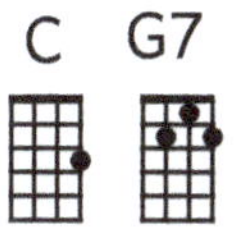

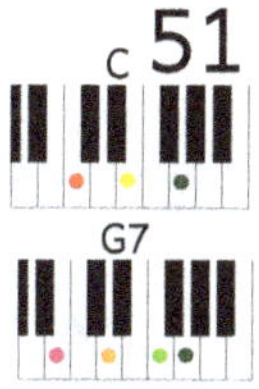

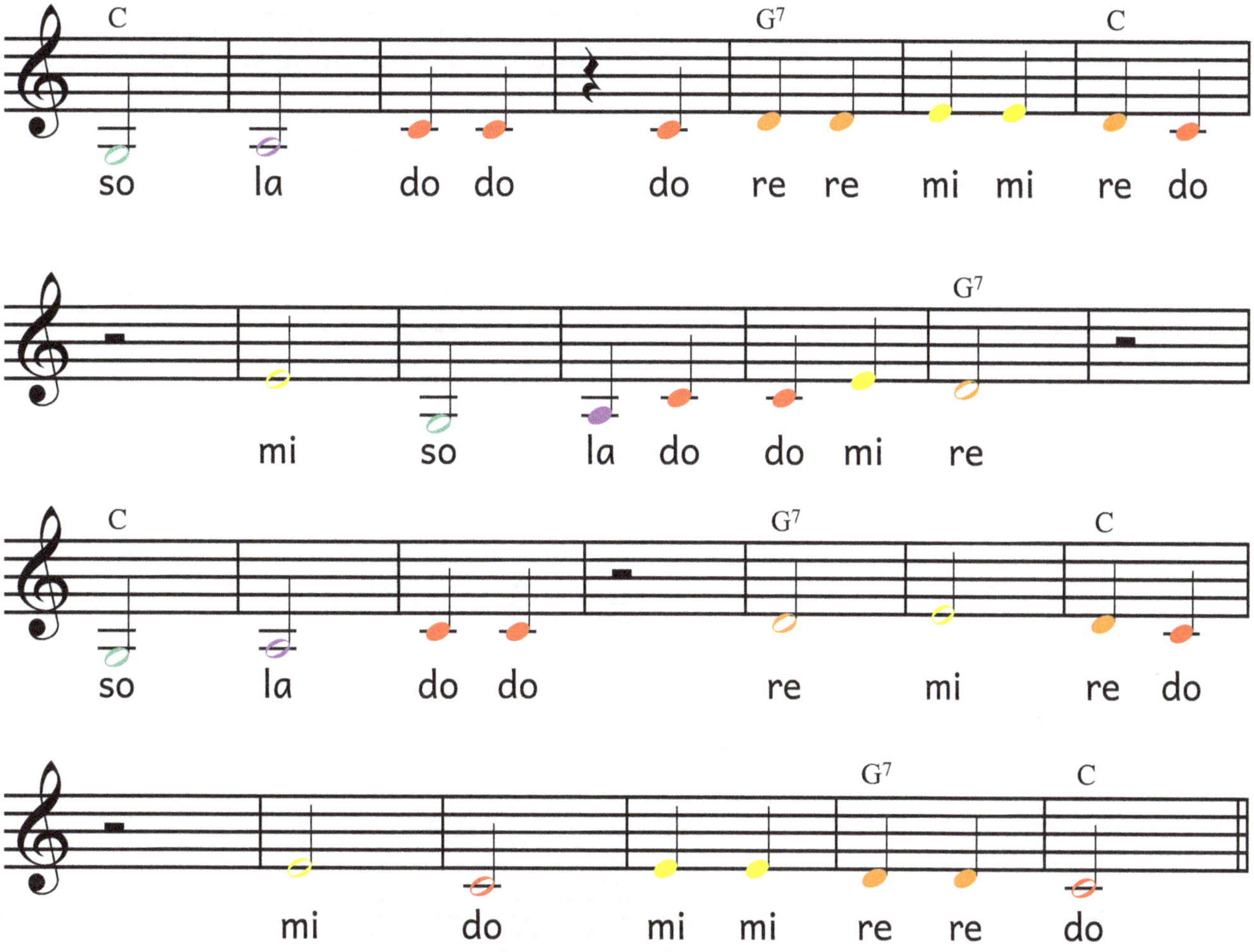

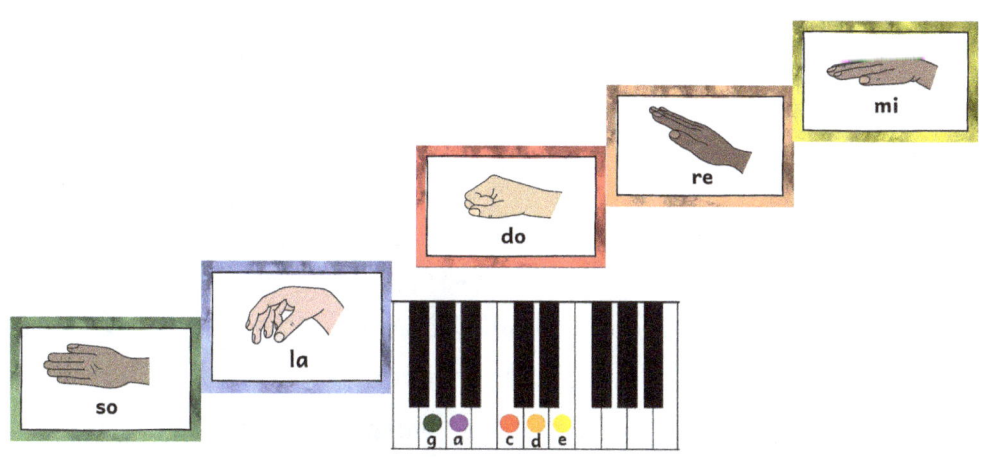

Español
Queremos Justicia en Nuestro Mundo
Music: Spiritual (Oh! Oh! Freedom)

ke - ˈre - mos hu - ˈsti-sja.   kwi - ˈða-mos   ˈu-nos ðe
Que - re - mos ju - sti-cia.   Cui - da-mos   u-nos de

ˈo - tros.   ke - ˈre - mos hu - ˈsti sja en ˈnwes-tro ˈmun-do.
o-tros   Que - re - mos ju - sti-cia en nue-stro mun-do

a - ˈsi ke hu - ˈɣa-mos   ˈlim-pjo   i   ˈmos-tra-mos kwi-
A - si que ju - ga-mos lim-pio   y   mo-stra-mos cui-

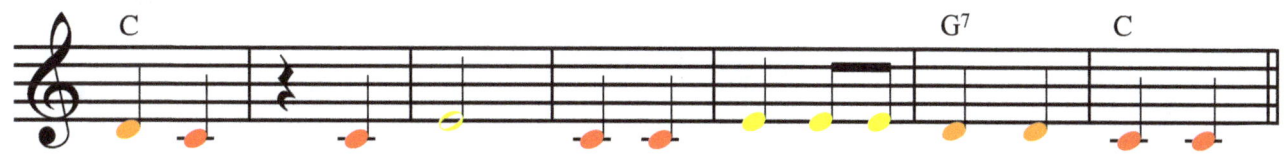

ˈða - ðo.   ke - ˈre - mos hu - ˈsti-sja en ˈnwes-tro ˈmun-do
da-do   Que - re - mos ju - sti-cia en nue-stro mun-do

Copyright © 2024 Sarah Samuelson Studio

Lesson 18: do-re-mi-so-la
You are Important
Music: England (Here Comes a Bluebird)

so so so la so mi mi so so la so mi

mi mi re re do mi mi do

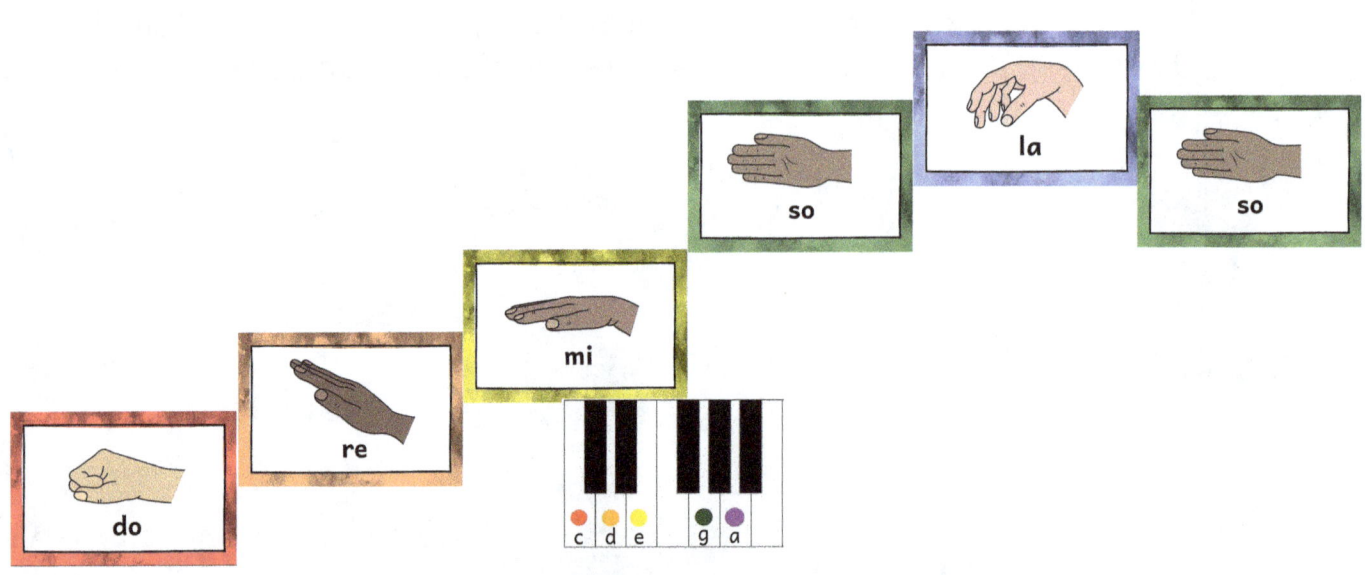

Copyright © 2024 Sarah Samuelson Studio

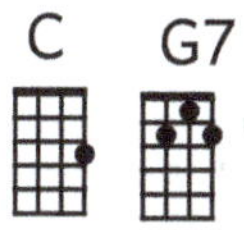

English
You are Important
Music: England (Here Comes a Bluebird)

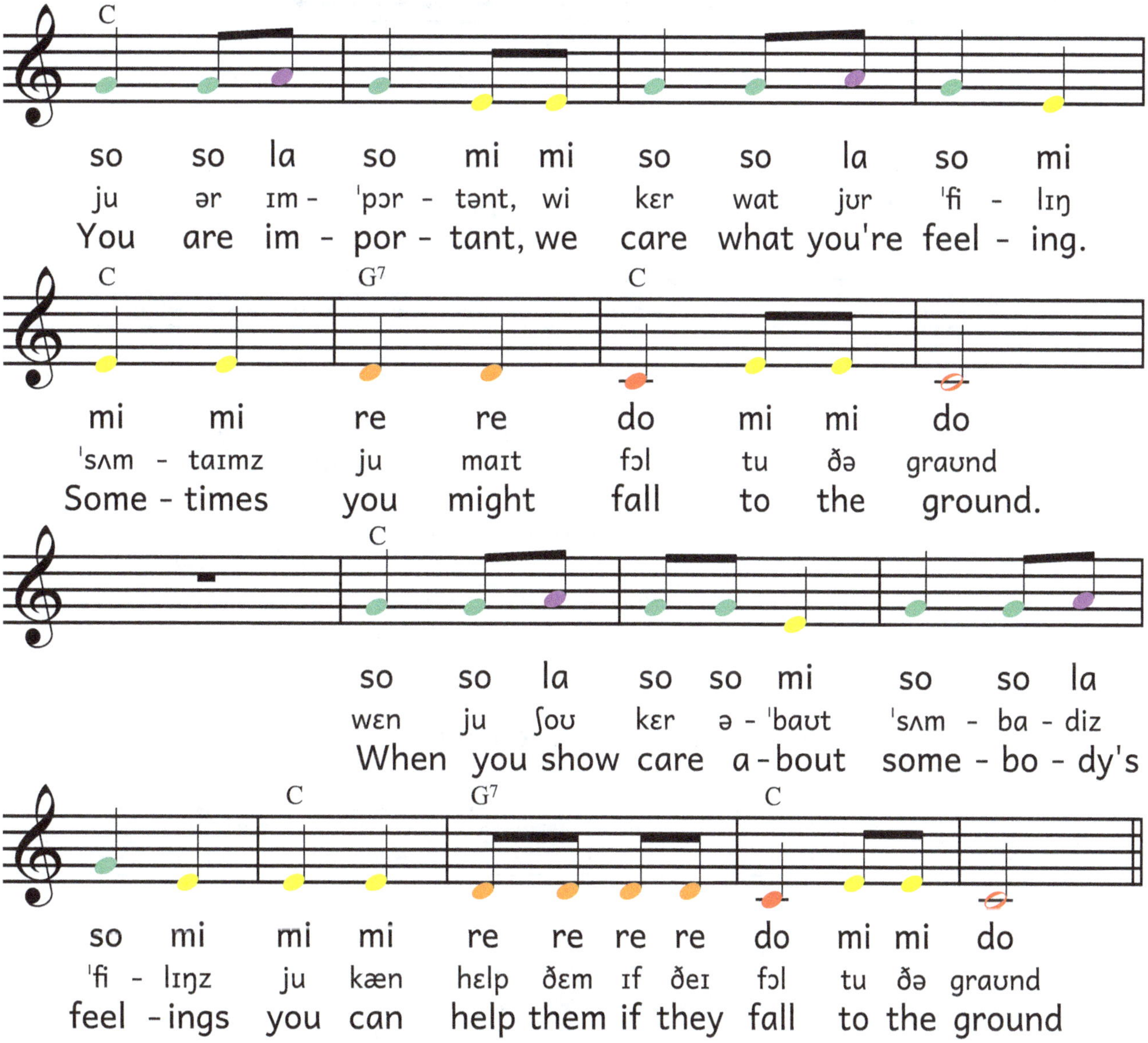

so so la so mi mi so so la so mi
ju ər ɪm-ˈpɔr-tənt, wi kɛr wat jʊr ˈfi-lɪŋ
You are im-por-tant, we care what you're feel-ing.

mi mi re re do mi mi do
ˈsʌm-taɪmz ju maɪt fɔl tu ðə graʊnd
Some-times you might fall to the ground.

so so la so so mi so so la
wɛn ju ʃoʊ kɛr ə-ˈbaʊt ˈsʌm-ba-diz
When you show care a-bout some-bo-dy's

so mi mi mi re re re re do mi mi do
ˈfi-lɪŋz ju kæn hɛlp ðɛm ɪf ðeɪ fɔl tu ðə graʊnd
feel-ings you can help them if they fall to the ground

Traditional lyrics:
Here comes a blue bird
through the window,
Hi-did-dle-dum day day day.

Copyright © 2024 Sarah Samuelson Studio

Español
Eres importante
Music: England (Here Comes a Bluebird)

'e - res im - por -'tan - te nos im -'por - ta 'ko - mo te 'sjen - tes in -
E - res im - por - tan - te, nos im - por - ta co - mo te sien - tes in -

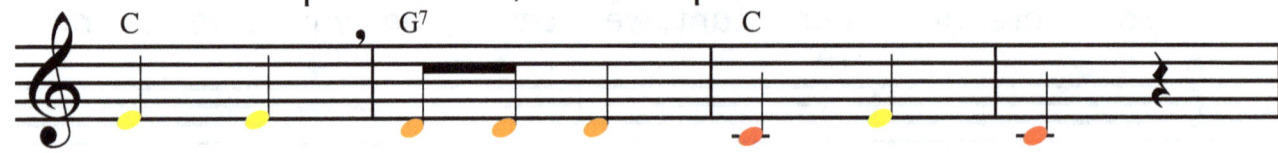

'klu - so si ka - es al sue - lo
clu - so si ca - es al sue - lo.

'kwan - do te pre - o - ku - pas por sus sen - ti - mjen - tos
Cuan - do te pre - o - cu - pas por sus sen - ti - mien - tos,

'pwe - ðes a - ju -'ðar - les si ka -'en al 'swe - lo
pue - des a - yu - dar - les si ca - en al sue - lo

Copyright © 2024 Sarah Samuelson Studio

Lesson 19: do-re-mi-so
We Can Learn to Express Our Emotions
Music: Argentina (Los elefantes)

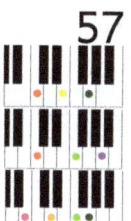

so so fa mi mi mi   so so so fa mi mi   so so la so fa mi

fa mi re   fa fa fa mi re re   fa fa mi

re re re   so so so fa mi re   mi re do

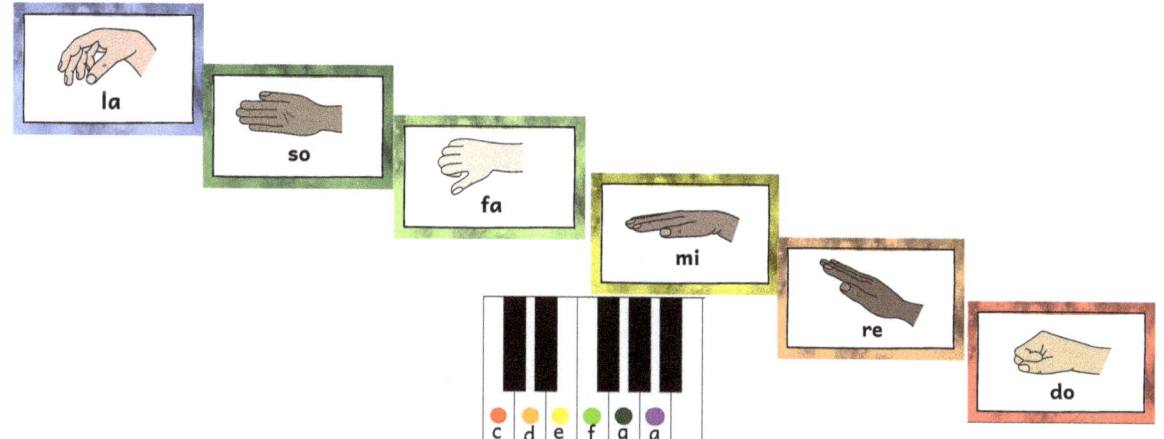

Copyright © 2024 Sarah Samuelson Studio

Español
Aprendemos a expresar emociones
Music: Argentina (Los elefantes)

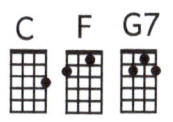

a - pren - ˈde - mos   a   ek - spre - ˈsar   e - mo - ˈsjo - nes
A - pren - de - mos   a   ex - pre - sar   e - mo - cio - nes.

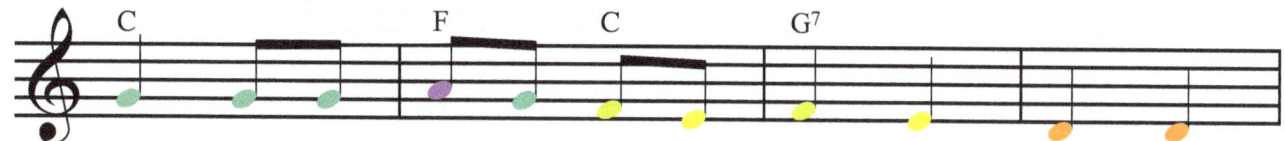

kon - ˈstrwi - mos   a - mi - ˈsta - ðes   sa - lu - ˈda - bles
Con - strui - mos   a - mi - sta - des   sa - lu - da - bles.

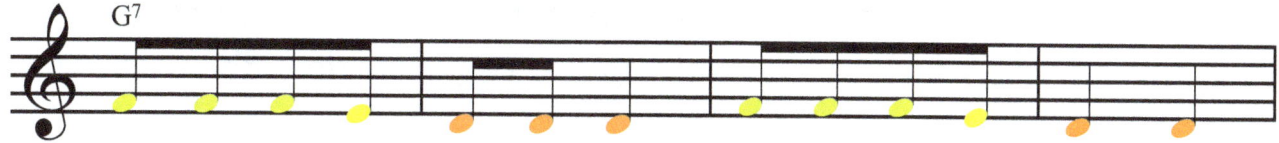

ˈkwan - do   ˈso - mos   kon - θjen - ˈtes   e - mo - ˈsjo - nal - men - te
Cuan - do   so - mos   con - sien - tes   e - mo - cio - nal - men - te,

po - ˈde - mos em - pa - ti - ˈzar__   i   es - ku - ˈtʃar
po - de - mos em - pa - ti   zar__   y   e - scu - char.

Traditional Argentinian Song: Los Elefantes

un e le ˈfã te se βa lan se_a βa   so βre la te la ðe_u na ra ɲa
Un elefante se balance aba   sobre la tela de_una_araña

ko mo βe i a ke re si sti a fwe a ɟa ma ra_o tro_e le fã nte
Como veîa,   que resistía, fué a llamarra_otro_elefante.

One elephant was balancing on a spider web
How he saw that it resisted weight he went to call another elephant.

Copyright © 2024 Sarah Samuelson Studio

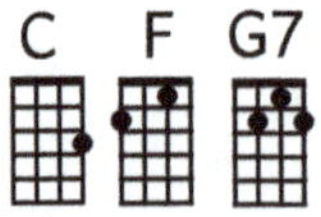

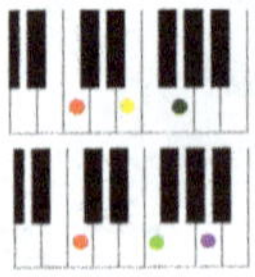

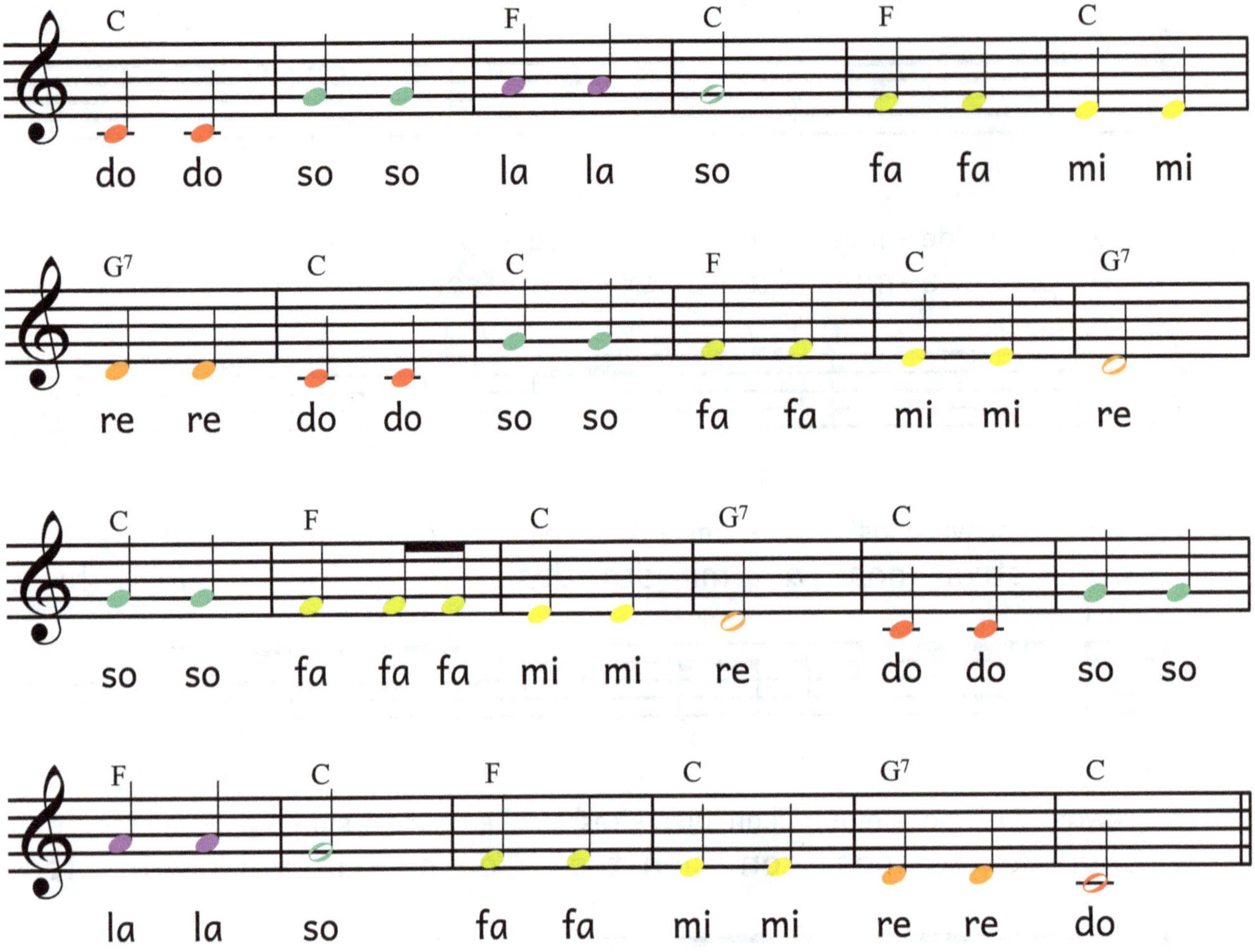

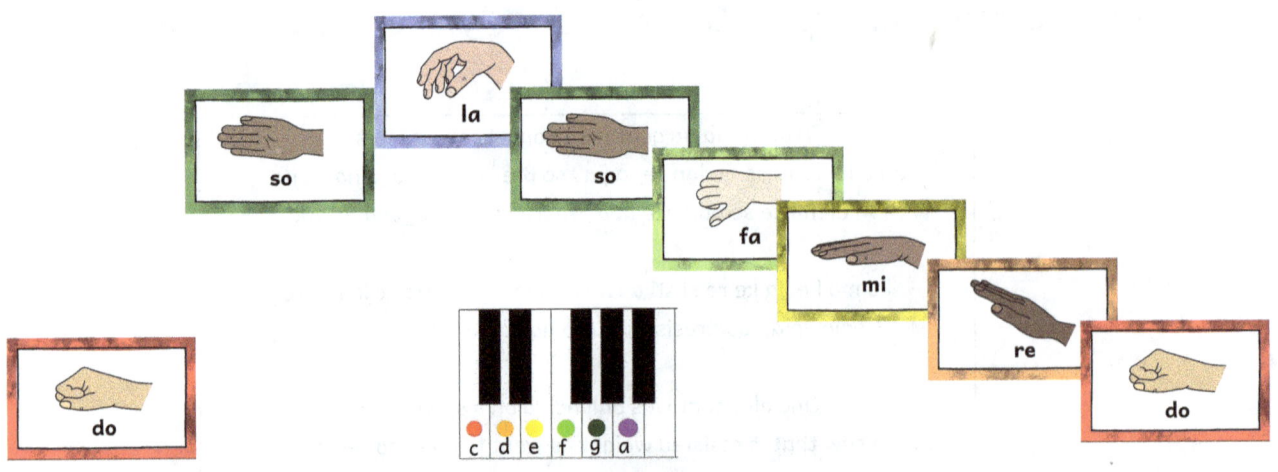

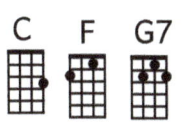

English
We are Like Stars in the Night
Music: Twinkle Twinkle Little Star

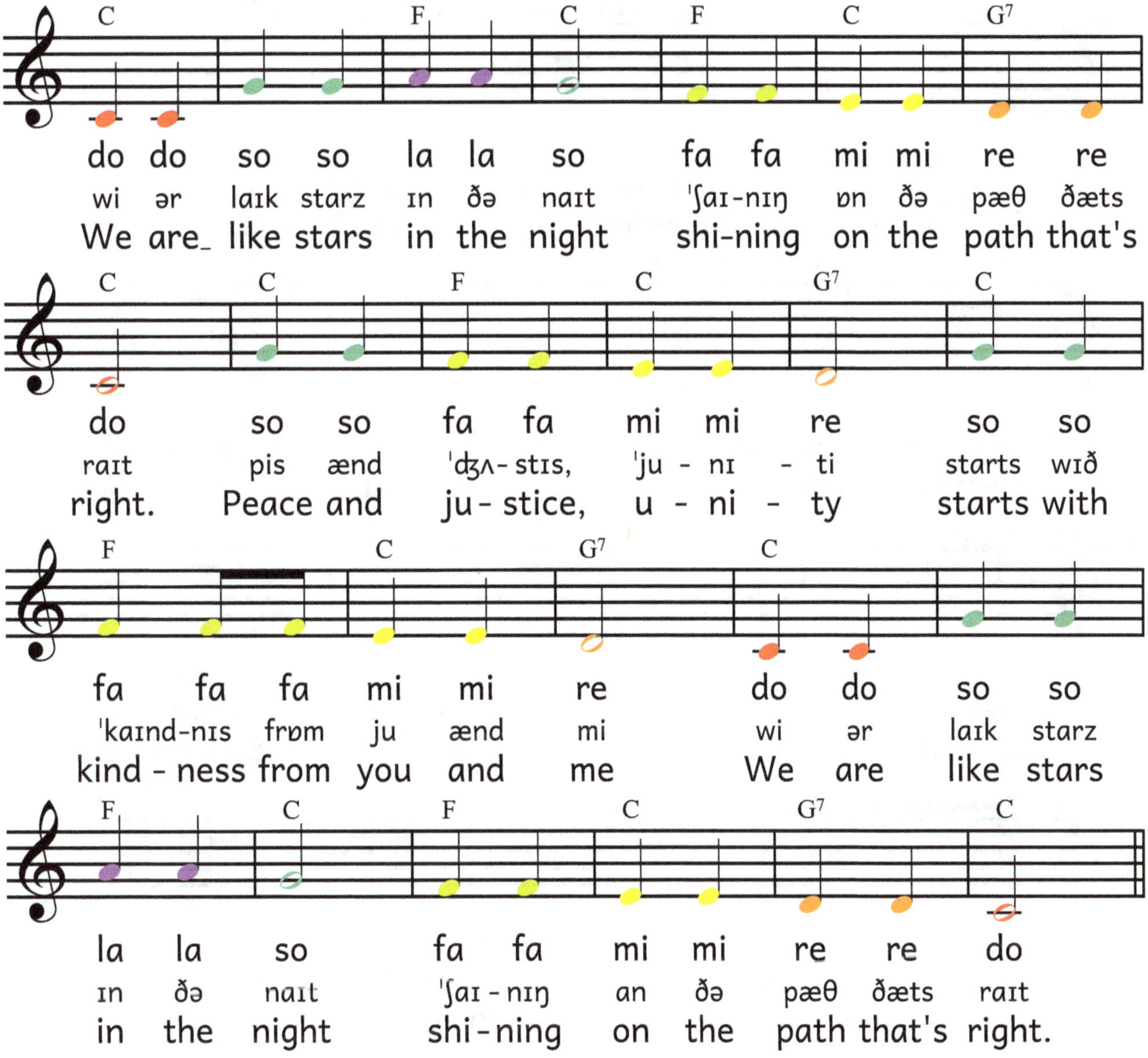

Español
Somos como estrella en la Noche
Music: Twinkle Twinkle Little Star

so - mos ˈko - mo e - ˈstrɛ - ʎas en la ˈno - tʃe, bri - ˈʎan - do en el ka -
So - mos co - mo e - stre - llas en la no - che, bri - llan - do en el ca -

ˈmi - no ko - ˈrɛk - to pas i hu - ˈsti - sja, la u - ni - ˈðad ko
mi - no co - rrec - to. Paz y ju - sti - cia, la u - ni - dad, co -

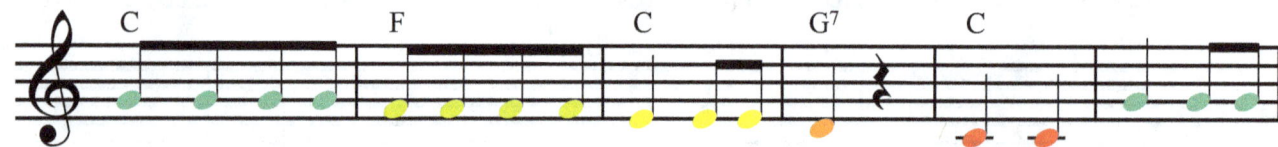

ˈmjen - sa kon a ma - βi - ˈlað de ti i de mi so - mos ˈko - mo e -
mien - za con a - ma - bi - lad de ti i de mí So - mos co - mo e -

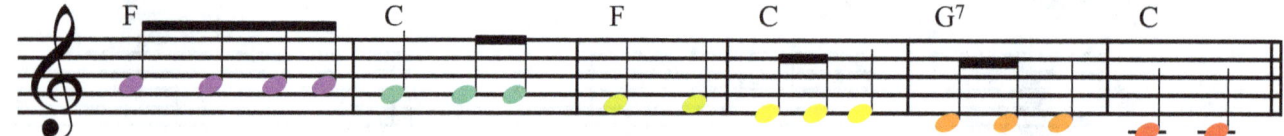

ˈstrɛ - ʎas en la ˈno - tʃe, bri - ˈʎan - do en el ka - ˈmi - no ko - ˈrɛk - to
stre - llas en la no - che, bri - llan - do en el ca - mi - no co - rrec - to

Copyright © 2024 Sarah Samuelson Studio

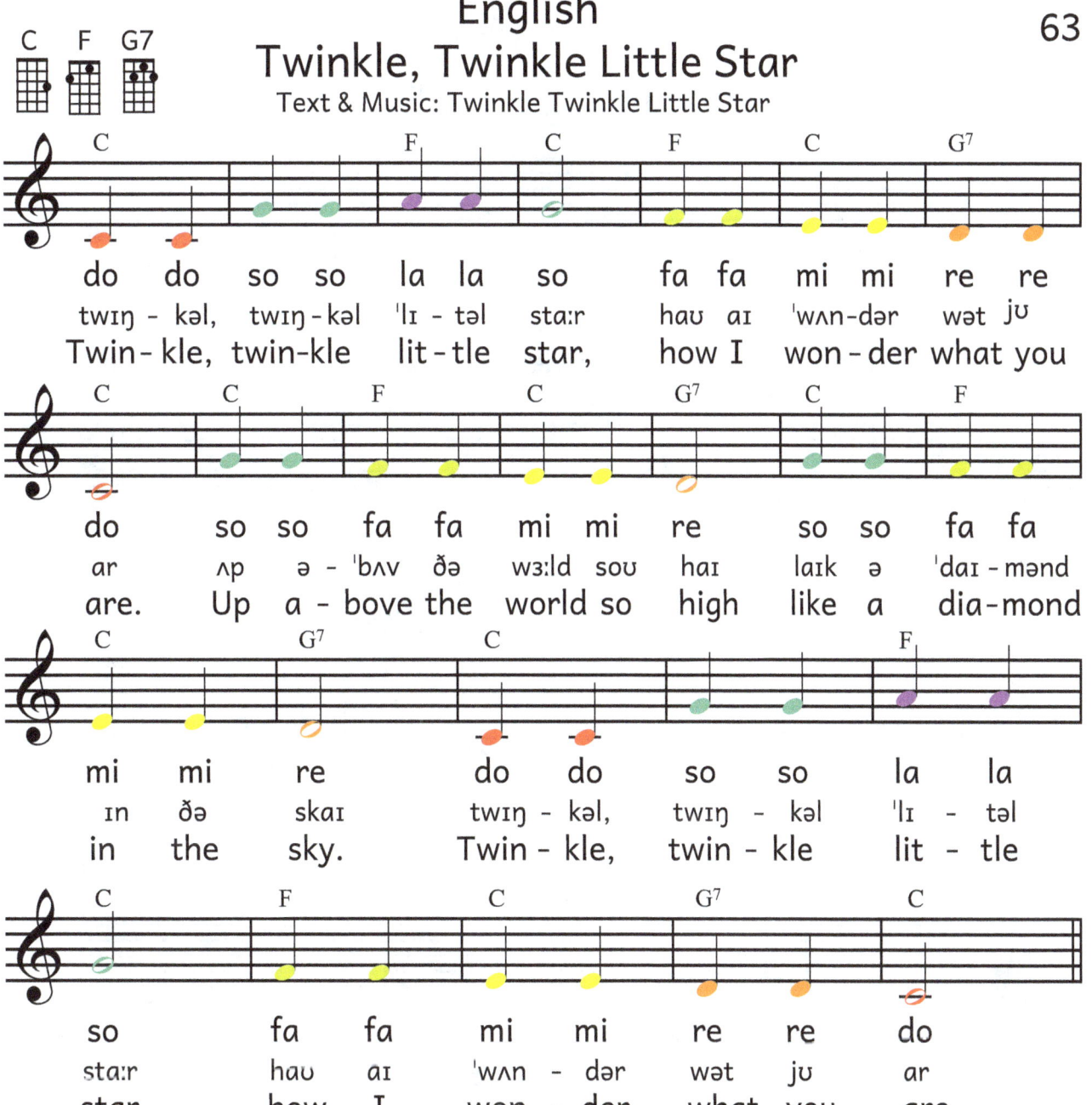

Español
Estrellita Donde Estas?

es - tre - 'ʎi - ta 'ðon-de es - 'tas me pre - 'ɣun - to
Es - tre - lli - ta don-de es - tás? Me pre - gun - to

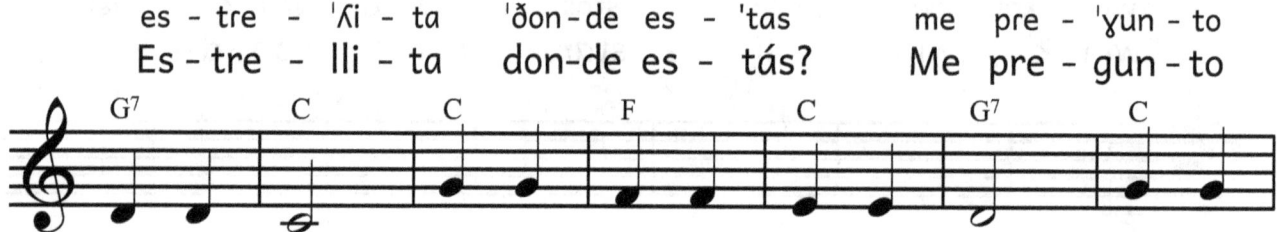

ke se - 'ras en el 'sje - lo jen el mar un dja -
qué se - rás En el cie - lo y en el mar un dia -

man - 'te ðe βer - 'ðað es - tre - 'ʎi - ta 'ðon-de es -
man - te de ver - dad Es - tre - lli - ta don-de es -

'tas me pre - 'ɣun - to 'ke se - 'ras
tás? Me pre - gun - to qué se - rás

> Translation of Spanish
> Little star, where are you?
> I wonder what you are.
> In the sky and in the sea
> A real diamond
> Little star, where are you?
> I wonder what you are.

Copyright © 2024 Sarah Samuelson Studio

Français
Ah! vous dirai-je, Maman

Translation of French:
Oh! Shall I tell you, Mommy
What is bothering me?
Daddy wants me to reason
like a grown-up person,
Me, I say that sweets
Are worth more than reasoning.

Lesson 21: so-la
We All Have a Super Power
Music: Mexico (Chocolate molinillo)

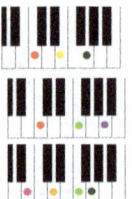

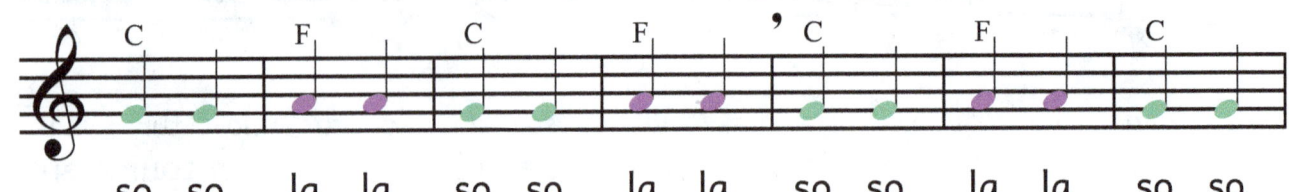

so so la la so so la la so so la la so so

la la so so mi fa so mi fa so so mi fa so fa mi re do do

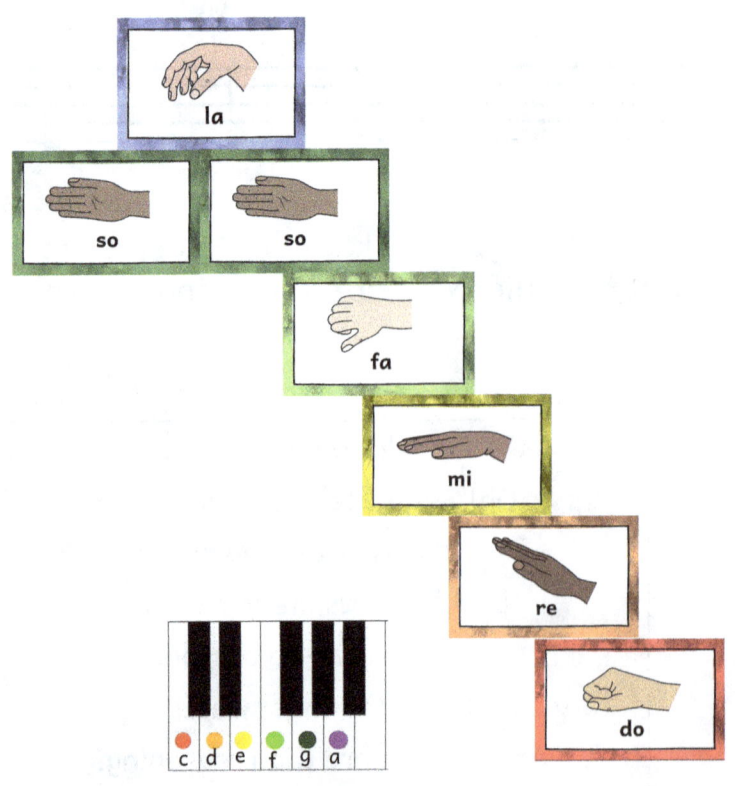

Copyright © 2024 Sarah Samuelson Studio

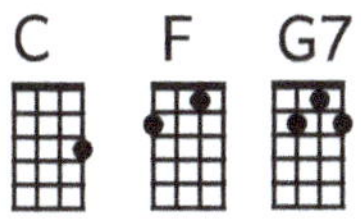

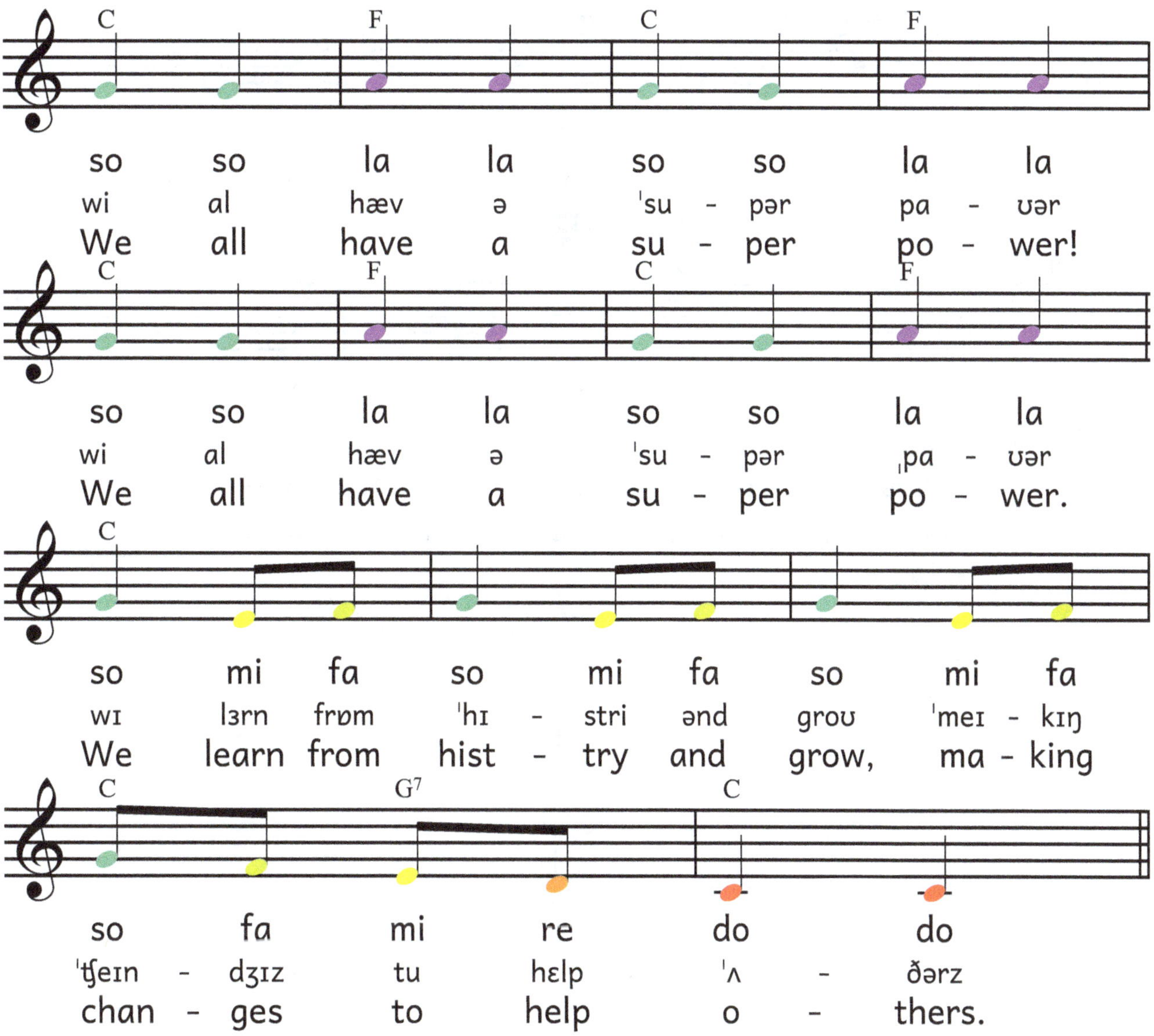

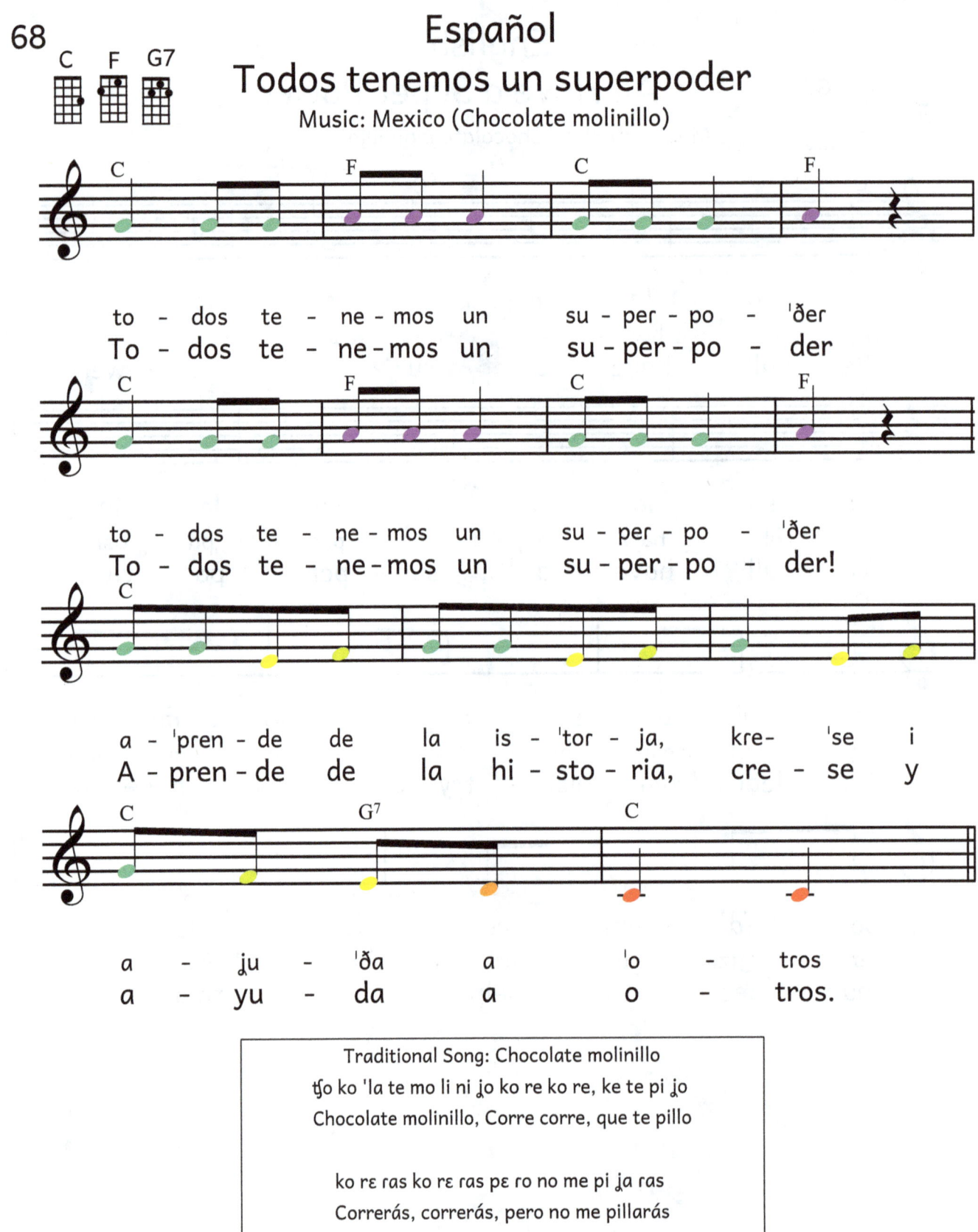

C F G7

Lesson 22: do-re-mi-fa

I am Learning to Regulate

Music: Japan (Kaeru nota ga)

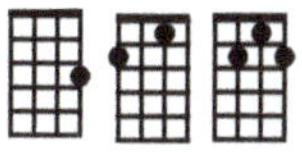

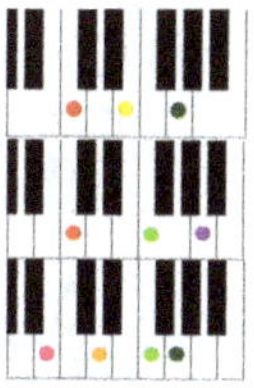

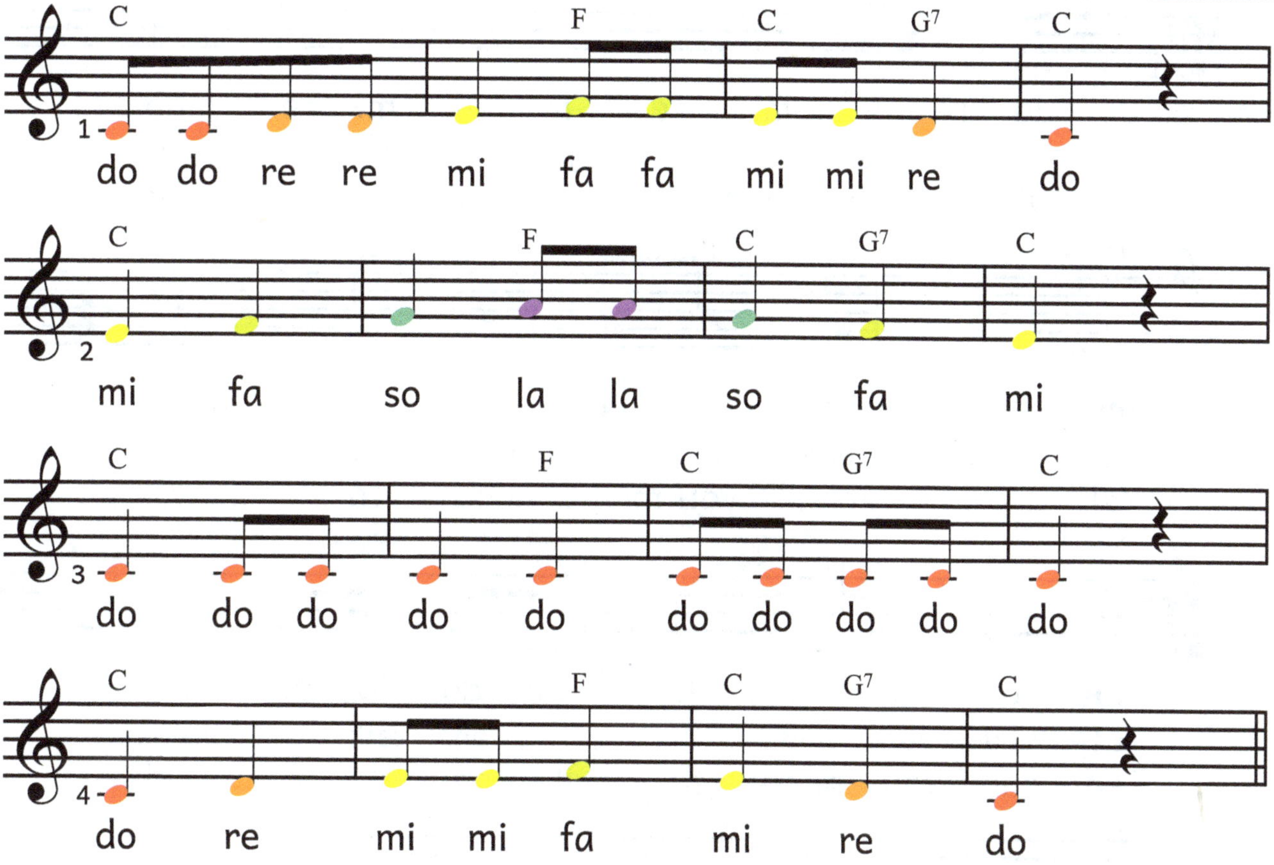

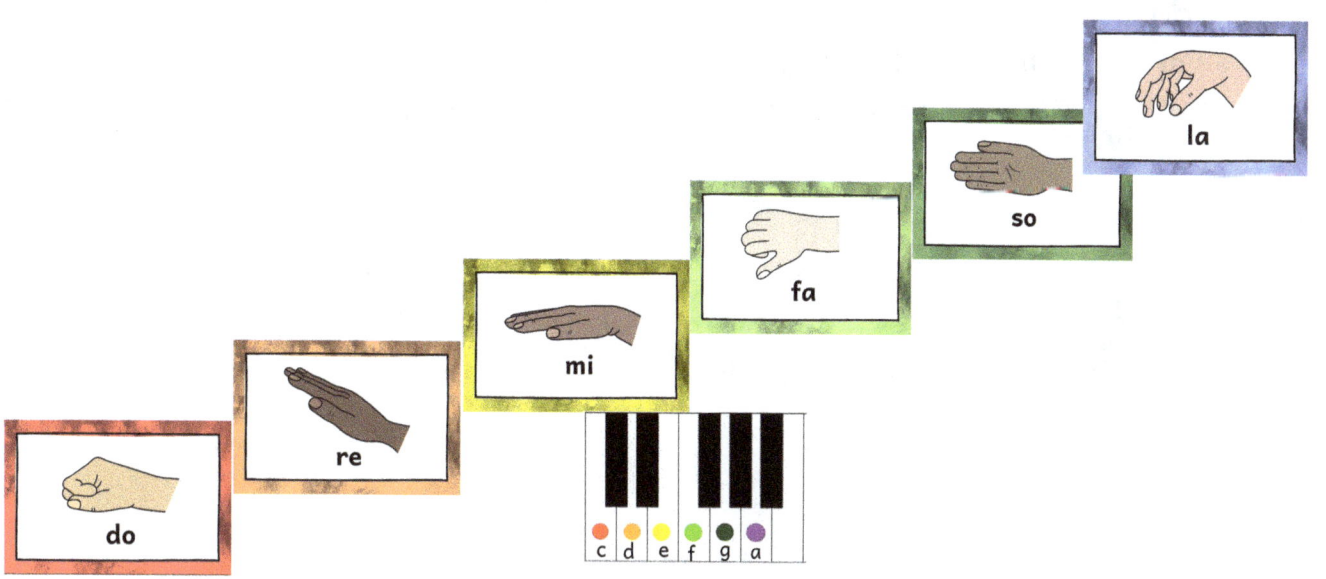

Español
Estoy aprendiendo a regularme
Music: Japan (Kaeru nota ga)

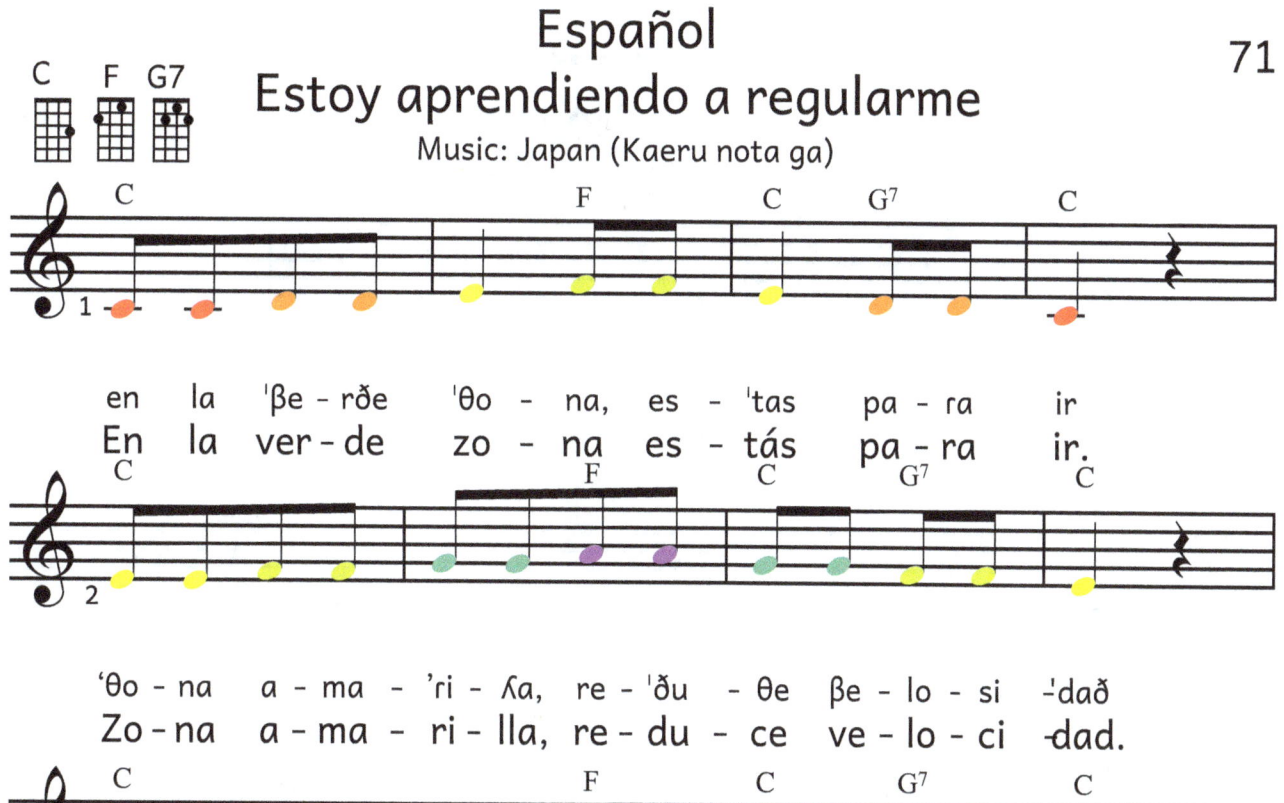

Japanese
Kaeru No Uta
Text & Music: Japan

Translation of Japanese:
The frog's song
we can hear it.
Gwa is like a frog sound.

Copyright © 2024 Sarah Samuelson Studio

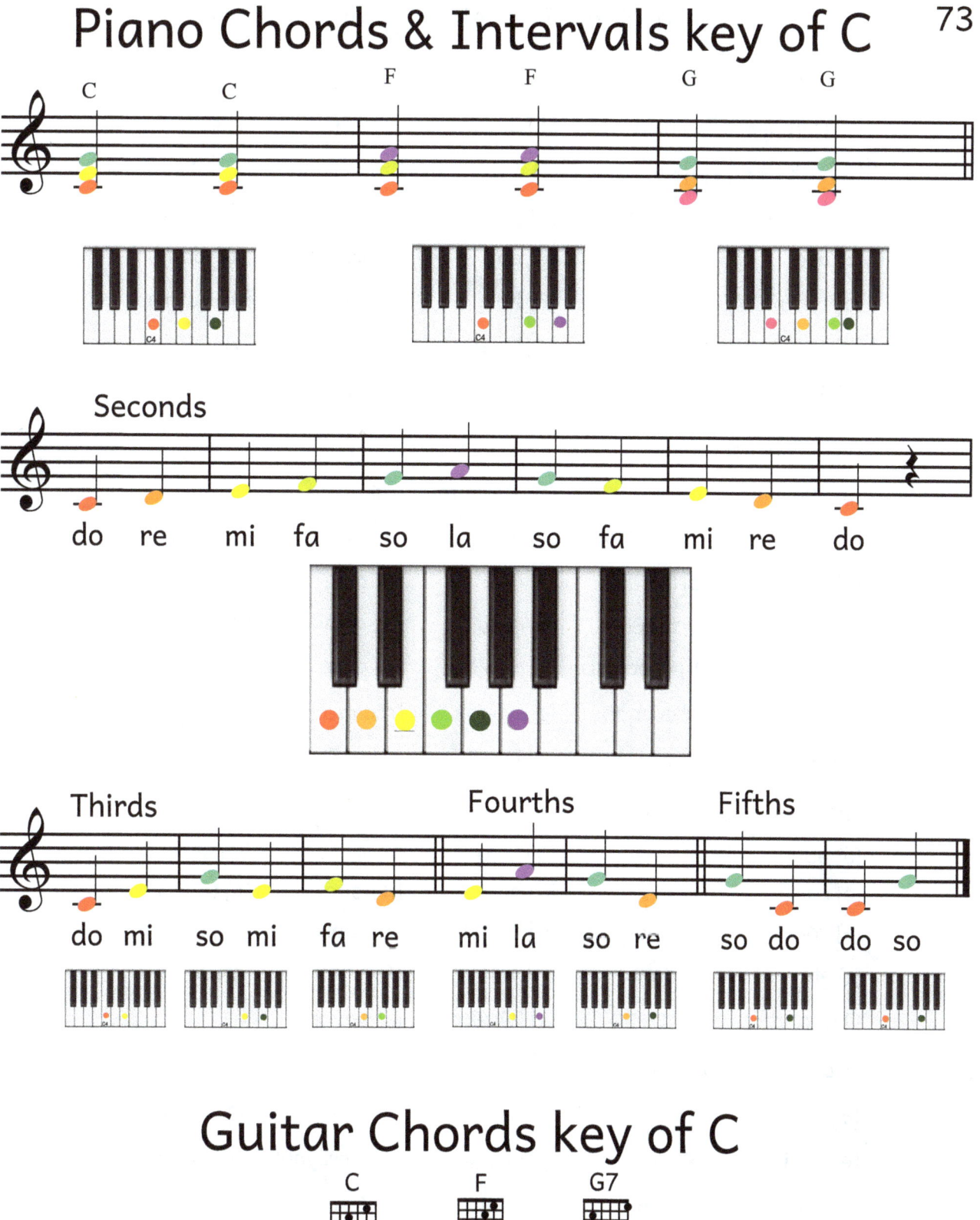

International Phonetic Alphabet Guides

IPA – English version

[ɑ] October	[o] okay	[d] day	[l] last	[ʃ] shoe
[æ] ask	[ɔ] all	[f] few	[m] me	[j] yet
[e] vacation	[u] school	[ʒ] genre	[n] nest	[θ] three
[ɛ] bed	[ʊ] good	[g] go	[ŋ] sing	[t] today
[ə] taken	[ʌ] up	[h] how	[p] place	[ð] mother
[i] we	[b] be	[dʒ] just	[ɹ] right	[v] voice
[ɪ] if	[tʃ] child	[k] kite	[s] say	[w] when

IPA – Español version

[a] chocolate	[j] rey	[ã] elefante	[l] lino	[s] saco
[e] bebé	[w] cuatro	[ẽ] amen	[m] madre	[θ] cereal
[ɛ] bendito	[b] bestia	[f] fase	[n] nido	[t] tía
[ə] taken	[β] braβo	[g] gato	[ɲ] mañana	[x] ojo
[i] di, y	[tʃ] chocolate	[ɣ] siɣno	[p] pozo	[ʎ] caballo
[o] sol	[d] cuando	[j̞] ayuno	[r] carro	
[u] su	[ð] dádiva	[k] kilo	[ɾ] braβo	

IPA – Brazilian Português

[a] aqui	[o] você	[ĩ] cinco	[ʒ] vejo	[ɾ] cara
[ɐ] coisa	[ɔ] só	[õ] bom	[j] noite	[ɲ] tenho
[e] você	[u] tudo	[ũ] mundo	[w] quase	[dʒ] cidade
[ɛ] até	[ẽ] dança	[g] algo	[ʎ] filho	[tʃ] noite
[i] isso	[ẽ] tempo	[ʃ] baixo	[ʁ] ser	

IPA – Kreyòl-Ayisyen

[a] pale	[i] li	[u] ou	[œ̃] tan	[ʃ] chita
[e] beni	[ɔ] kom	[y] plume	[ɛ̃] incroyable	[tʃ] chicken
[ɛ] Senyè	[o] opere	[õ] kontan	[ʒ] Jesus	[j] yereswa
[ə] je				

Bibliography

Books

Adler, D. (1996). *The Kids' Catalog of Jewish Holidays.* Jewish Publication Society.

Bronstein, H. (1974). *A Passover Haggadah.* Central Conference of American Rabbis.

Burleigh, H.T. *Negro Spirituals arranged by H.T. Burleigh.* Art Song Central.

Campbell, P. (2014). *Music in Childhood from Preschool through the Elementary Grades.* Cengage Learning.

Carpenter, D. (2001). *African American Heritage Hymnal: 575 Hymns, Spirituals, and Gospel Songs.* GIA Publications.

Church of God in Christ Publishing Board. (1982). *Yes, Lord! Hymnal.* Church of God in Christ Publishing House.

Emmerson, J. (2014). *The Complete Illustrated Children's Bible.* Harvest House Publishers.

Hayes, R. (1948). *My Songs Panels 1, 2 & 3.* Little Brown and Company.

Giovanni, N. (2009). *On my journey now: Looking at African-American history through the spirituals.* Candlewick Press.

Glover, S. (1845) *History of the Norwich Sol-fa.* Norwich: Jarrold & Sons.

Musleah, R. (1999). *Why On This Night: A Passover Haggadah for Family Celebration.* Simon & Schuster.

Nicholls, K. (2020). *My Favourite Bible Stories For Children Around the World.* Harper Collins Publishers.

Orozco, J. (1994). *De Colores and Other Latin-American Folk Songs.* Puffin Books.

Various. (2002). *The Complete Jewish Songbook.* Transcontinental Music Publications.

White, C. (2006). *Tryin' to Get Ready: 30 African American Spirituals Arranged for SATB Voices.* GIA Publications.

Wilcox, C. (2003). *He Mele Aloha: A Hawaiian Songbook.* 'Oli'Oli Productions, L.L.C.

Zondervan. (2005). *The Beginner's Bible.* Zonderkidz.

Bibles

Aramaic Peshitta New Testament Translation. (2006). Light of the Word Ministry.

Bauscher, G. (2007) *HPBT Holy Peshitta Bible Translation.* Lulu Publishing.

Smith, J. (1876) *Smith Literal Translation.* Hartford American Publishing Co.

Websites:

www.bethsnotesplus.com

www.biblehub.com

www.mamalisa.com

www.easypronunciation.com

www.internationalphoneticassociation.org

www.ipanow.com

www.michaelkravchuk.com

www.stepbible.org

Special Thanks to Individuals

Katie African at Fivrr - Book Front & Back Covers

Daniele Leano - Português pronunciation

Priscilla Ozodo-Acevedo - voice coach and friend who has encouraged me so much in this project

Marie Polynice – Kreyòl Ayisyen (Haitian-Creole)

Christina Sanchez – Español pronunciation and sister and friend

Andriana Seay – voice coach and friend who has also encouraged me and helped me with singing

My wonderful husband, daughters, parents and sisters!

About Sarah Samuelson

Sarah Samuelson earned a Bachelor in Music Education from the University of Puget Sound, a Masters in Music Ed from Minnesota State Univ, and National Board Certification in Early Childhood Music Education. She has 15 years experience teaching music education in public schools and 6 years of teaching music education courses at the University of Puget Sound. She shared the ways that she adapted curriculum for the music classes for special education students she taught and for students with 504 plans. She has also used her skills in languages to meet needs of multilingual learners. In her private studio, Sarah has continued to learn from students with special needs, including students with Autism spectrum disorder, Trisomy 21 (Down syndrome), and students with language impairment. Combining these areas of knowledge and experience, Sarah created Learn to Sing in Harmony, a song-based method with an empathy theme to learn to read music for schools and homeschool learning. The curriculum is based on Kodaly method and incorporating folk songs from many different countries and African American spirituals from the United States and notes use the colors of the popular boomwhackers and recorders. Learn to Sing in Harmony Bible version for Christian-based learning and it follows the stories in multiple children's Bibles so that there is a song for every story. Since 2020 she has been participating in monthly Courageous Conversations (based on the Glenn Singleton book and curriculum) led by Dr. Connie Sims, reading books and watching movies and documentaries to increase her awareness and understanding of racial inequality. The books have four levels and progress in music theory with the goal being the joy of harmony! Sarah studied classical singing in her undergrad and grad programs and has performed in operas and musicals. She has been continuing her vocal growth learning new technique from vocal coaches, Onyedikachi Priscilla Ozodo-Acevedo and Andriana Seay, to sing outside of the classical genre and style especially in the areas of multiethnic & gospel worship and jazz.

More Learn to Sing & Play in Harmony Books

Learn to Sing Bible Versions

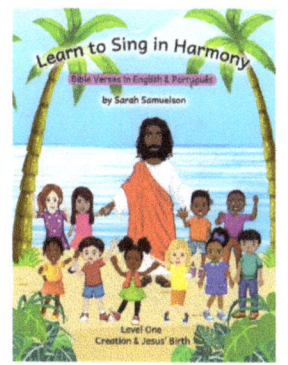 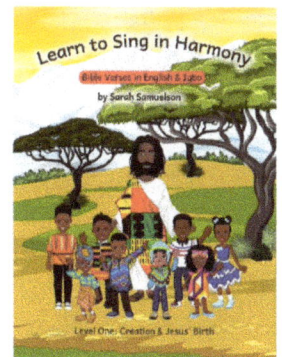 

Learn to Play Recorder Books

Empathy Books for Schools

  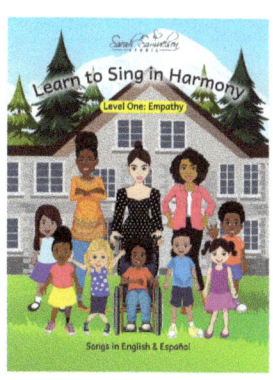 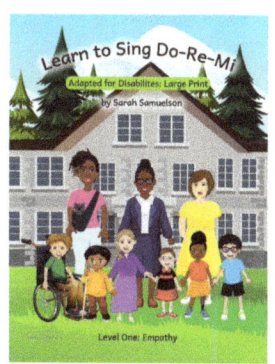

Jump-start Versions

Adapted for Disabilities

 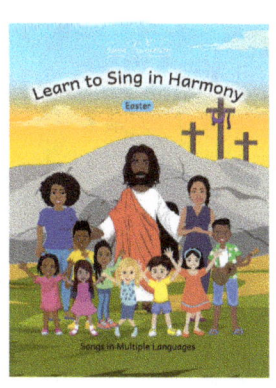  

Date	Assignment	M	T	W	Th	F	S	S

Date	Assignment	M	T	W	Th	F	S	S
		M	T	W	Th	F	S	S

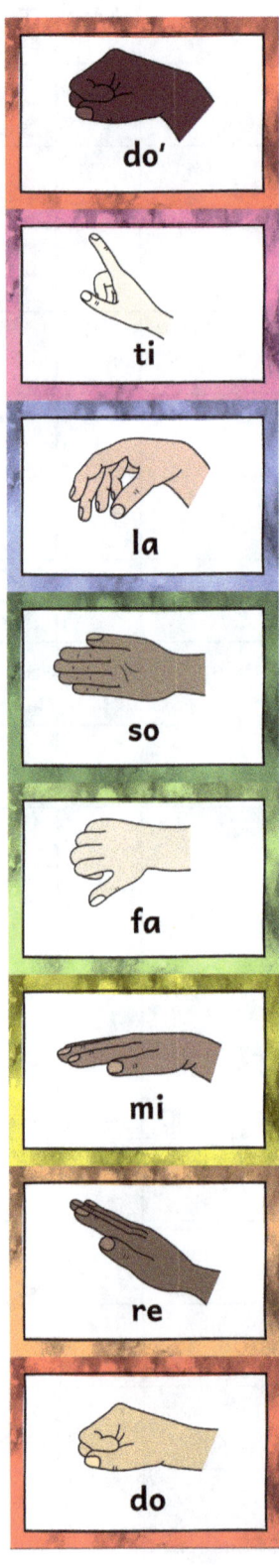

Copyright © 2024 Sarah Samuelson Studio
All Rights Reserved.

No part of this publication may be reproduced or transmitted in any form without permission from the publisher.

www.ingramcontent.com/pod-product-compliance
Lightning Source LLC
Chambersburg PA
CBHW080416170426
43194CB00015B/2825